IT COULD
ONLY HAPPEN
TO ME

To Kim!
   I hope this makes
   you laugh!

      Shaun Hickey

IT COULD ONLY HAPPEN TO ME

A MEMOIR

SHARON ANN HICKEY

IT COULD ONLY HAPPEN TO ME
A MEMOIR

iUniverse books may be ordered through booksellers or by contacting:

iUniverse
1663 Liberty Drive
Bloomington, IN 47403
www.iuniverse.com
1-800-Authors (1-800-288-4677)

Because of the dynamic nature of the Internet, any web addresses or links contained in this book may have changed since publication and may no longer be valid. The views expressed in this work are solely those of the author and do not necessarily reflect the views of the publisher, and the publisher hereby disclaims any responsibility for them.

Any people depicted in stock imagery provided by Thinkstock are models, and such images are being used for illustrative purposes only.
Certain stock imagery © Thinkstock.

ISBN: 978-1-4917-5836-6 (sc)
ISBN: 978-1-4917-5838-0 (hc)
ISBN: 978-1-4917-5837-3 (e)

Library of Congress Control Number: 2015900523

Printed in the United States of America.

iUniverse rev. date: 02/09/2015

CONTENTS

PREFACE

I know there is a rich person trying to get out of this body. Maybe my funny stories will make it happen. If nothing else, maybe someone out there will realize his or her luck isn't so bad after all!

I have always had funny and unusual things happen to me. I call them my "Sharon stories." My dad told me more than thirty years ago that I should be writing a book. Over the years, I have kept little notes about these events, and I stored them in my computer desk. My children were warned not to disturb them, as someday I was going to "do something with them." That day has come.

I have several reasons for writing this book. First of all, I want to memorialize these funny events that have been part of my life. Second, I would like to share them with others. In this book I have compiled humorous tales about vacations, children, husbands, dining out, and just normal everyday activities (normal for everyone else, that is!)

I have always been able to laugh at these experiences, and when I share them with my friends and family, they enjoy them too. That encouraged me to reach a larger audience. Through the years, I have entertained at various social events at my church and other places. And for more than forty years, I have shared these stories with my longtime friend Debi, who lives in Florida. We started out as pen pals when we were teens, and I still share my tales through snail mail today, with an occasional text message to Debi here and there. (That's a lot of postage!)

One time I even entered a competition at Go Bananas Comedy Club for amateur night and won! I didn't even mind that the trophy had the wrong date on it. That was just another story to add to my collection.

My hope is that anyone who has ever had a bad day will be able to relate to my tales of woe and smile.

This book is dedicated to my family for being able to laugh with me (or maybe at me) over the years and for allowing me to share humorous stories about them as well.

I would like to thank God for giving me a sense of humor and the opportunity to share these amusing events with a reading audience.

INTRODUCTION

I don't just have a black cloud that follows me—I have the whole storm system! It started when I was pretty young. Maybe the dream I had as a young adult was a premonition: I dreamed that I was at my mom's with a bunch of ladies. It was Christmas, and we were opening presents. They all got beautiful robes, but when I opened my gift, I had a pair of sweat socks (probably dirty ones!) I am afraid to know the significance of that.

Many years ago, I was at the mall with my sister when we were approached by a lady who was conducting a survey. She totally ignored me, looked straight at my sister, and asked if we would be interested in participating. My sister said yes.

Without looking directly at me, just sort of nodding my way, the woman asked, "What about her?" My sister said yes, that I would be interested.

This whole scene was repeated as the woman proceeded to ask, "Are you over eighteen? What about her? Do you live within one hundred miles of Cincinnati? What about her? Do you do most of the grocery shopping for your home? What about her?" I was listening to this conversation and not even believing this woman. Why wouldn't she ask me a question or even acknowledge I was there?

Finally it was time to take us to the back area for the survey, and naturally my sister was asked to go first while I waited for my turn. After we both had completed the survey, my sister commented on what delicious chocolate desserts she got to sample. I love chocolate. I looked at her and said, "What chocolate desserts? All I had to sample were some not-so-delicious lemon-filled cakes." Thus began my stories.

CHAPTER 1

THREE SPOUSES AND A HOUSE

The first time I got married, my last name was Mote. Someone asked me once if I ever looked that up in the dictionary. I said no, and he proceeded to tell me that it means "insignificant speck." Well, that didn't surprise me. It won't surprise anyone else either. My first marriage ended in divorce, and when I would meet people I hadn't seen in a while, I would tell them I got *de*moted. This was especially funny when I said it at work and those who didn't know me overheard it. They had to wonder what terrible thing I did to get demoted, since that never happened at my job. The best thing I got from that marriage was my son Robert who was born in 1977. And I did have my name in lights once when I noticed the L was burned out in a MOTEL sign.

Eddie

This section is dedicated to my second husband, Eddie. We were married for twenty years, and we had two daughters, Rachel and Mandy. Eddie died in 2006, but he left us with fond memories and some very funny stories too.

I met Eddie at a dance in 1984. He was kind of shy, but nice. A friend of mine commented that he had pretty blue eyes. I said, "They are not blue; they are green." As it turned out, depending on which eye we were looking at, we were both right.

Eddie and I got married. We were excited when we found out we were going to be parents. I went for my doctor's appointment to find out whether we were having a girl or boy. I returned home and told Eddie it was going to be a girl. His response was, "Well, we still have a few months," like the baby could change into a boy. I don't think it works that way. Our daughter, Rachel, was born in June 1986.

Rachel was almost two when Eddie and I found out we were going to be parents again. We decided that our two-bedroom house was too small, though Eddie had already converted a small area off the living room into Rachel's room. Plus I wanted to get closer to my job, which was a forty-five-minute drive away. So we began looking for a bigger house. Our real estate lady was very nice, and we overlooked the fact that she kept calling Eddie "Andy." We looked at several houses before she showed us the last one.

I knew it was going to have issues when the Realtor said, "Not everyone would like this house." It had a sliding door instead of a front door, and cistern water, among other things.

And what did Eddie say? "I like this house!" After some deliberation and discussion, we decided to buy it.

So began the process of moving. I have found that most women like to plan ahead, where guys like to wait until the last minute to do things. That's how it was with packing. Finally we were down to the wire. When the movers came to take the big stuff, Eddie was still packing odds and ends. He told me to go ahead with the movers and said that he would finish up. Well, later when I was unpacking, I found the black garbage bags Eddie had put the last of the items in. I didn't dare reach down into them—he had packed razor blades and shoes in the same bag.

When we moved into our house, we only had one key. I went all over town trying to get a duplicate made with no luck. It was the exception to the rule that any key could be copied. Finally, I found a place that said they could do it. But I was also told maybe the new key would work, and maybe it wouldn't. I was willing to take the chance. I had a new one made, gave it to Eddie, and he lost it before we could even try it. It's one of those mysteries we will never know the answer to.

We moved from the west side of Cincinnati to the east side. We were in our house a few months when Eddie came home all excited. He said he found a new way to work that saved him twenty minutes in both directions. When I asked him about it, he said he went a different direction on I-275. Well, I guess once he cut out Indiana, the drive would be shorter.

I didn't know this at the time, but our town has a parade right before the fair each year. That first summer, while pregnant, I happened to go to the grocery store the day of the parade and made it almost back to our new home before I encountered road closures. I was unable to reach my street, which was right where the road was blocked. I was unfamiliar with the surrounding area, so I wasn't sure how to get home. I knew only one way, and I was not one to explore strange territory. It was not possible to just go around the block in our neighborhood; it's rural, and you could end up in the middle of nowhere. I didn't even know what the other end of my street looked like. I mean, why would I drive past my house?

I asked the policeman who was redirecting traffic how I could get home. He gave me quick directions and sent me on my way. The more I drove, the more scared I got. The houses got farther and farther apart, and I wasn't sure where I would end up. Not only was my car without air conditioning, but we were in the middle of a heat wave. I had a trunk full of groceries, including ice cream that was quickly melting. There were no cell phones at that time, so I was unable to call anyone. Even if I had been able to get a hold of Eddie, it wouldn't have done any good. He was worse at following directions than I was.

So here I was, a lost pregnant woman with a carload of groceries, trying to get home. I drove for a little while, and then I saw a man working on his motorcycle in his driveway. I decided to take my chances with this guy and hope he wasn't a serial killer waiting for his next victim. I pulled into his driveway and explained my situation. He gave me directions—several times—but he must have seen the confused look on my face because he finally told me to just follow him. So he jumped on his motorcycle, and I followed him to my house. When we both pulled in my driveway, the look on my husband's face was priceless. Poor Eddie!

When it came time for our second child together to be born, of course Eddie had already left for work. So my eleven-year-old son, Robert, called 911, and I waited. When the ambulance arrived, the staff was very nice and tried hard to get my mind off my pain. One of attendants asked me where I worked. I told her I worked for CG&E (Duke Energy now). She asked me which office, and I responded.

She then asked, "Oh, do you know Harry Winkler?" (The name was changed to protect the innocent).

I said, "Ewww—do you like him?"

And that's when she said in a not-so-nice voice, "Well, that's my father!"

Oh no! I thought. *What were the odds of this?* I think the lesson here is never ask a lady in labor a question that you don't want to know the answer to, because she will definitely tell you the truth. I thought she was going to open the ambulance doors and leave me on my own, but we made it to the nearest hospital without further incident (or conversation.)

Unfortunately, the hospital they took me to does not usually deliver babies. I was supposed to go to what I call the *real* hospital, where my doctor and nice birthing suite were waiting. But after being checked out by the doctors at this hospital, it was decided that there was no time to get me to the *real* hospital by ambulance. They said they would fly me by air-care. By the time that got arranged and I got over my fear of flying, I was told that wasn't happening, either. I was going to have the baby right where I was. Fine, I said, just bring me the drugs. No, I was told. It was too late for that. I was going to have the baby naturally.

Everyone was so excited that a baby was going to be born at this hospital that I think they were all in the delivery room with me—everyone, that is, except my husband. That poor guy. He was given so much conflicting information he wasn't sure which hospital to go to. Thank goodness he made it just in time. He was there when our daughter was born.

After Mandy came into the world, we were finally going to be taken by ambulance to the *real* hospital. I don't know the reason (maybe because they don't normally deliver babies), but my child was placed in what looked like bubble wrap for our trip there. Once we arrived, I found myself in what looked to me like a sub-basement.

After a few minutes a nurse came over and asked, "So honey, how far apart are your contractions?" When I answered that I had already had my baby, she said, "Oh. We knew where your baby was, but we didn't know where *you* were." Well, where did they *think* I would be?

Mandy was put in the nursery with a generic tag on her bed. There was no pink announcement like the other baby girls had. Also, since I didn't have her at that hospital, I did not get the birthing suite as planned. And when lunchtime came, I was forgotten.

A few years later, I wanted to get Mandy's birth certificate. I just knew there was going to be something weird about it. Sure enough, there was. No one seemed to know where it was—not the county, not the first hospital, and not the second one. I was told I was going to have to go to court with three witnesses who could verify that yes, I had been pregnant, and yes, I did have a baby on October 5. I really didn't want to have to do that, so I made one last attempt and called the first hospital again. This time the document was found—*stuck in a drawer!* I guess no one knew what else to do with it.

The House

My family moved to our house in 1988, and I still live there today.

The house is in a rural area, where mailboxes are frequently the victims of violence. Many times they are found destroyed and knocked off their post either by accident or because of a prank. One morning we found our mailbox badly damaged and lying in the ditch. We had already replaced it several times, so Eddie found a solution to our problem. He put big strips of Velcro on the bottom of the mailbox and on the post. That way, if and when our mailbox ever got hit again, it would just fall off the post without being destroyed, and we could just stick it back on. It worked. We never had to replace it again.

Eventually we got a post office box for our mail. Eddie was usually the one to collect the mail. One time I was the one getting the mail, and I ran into a friend of mine who worked in the post office. We got into a conversation, and she asked me what my husband looked like. Oh yeah—like I'm going to tell her! I mean, what if she matched him up with one of those wanted posters hanging on the post office wall? As my stories will reveal, he was a person to be worried about!

We do not have city water out here; the house has a cistern. This became a problem whenever Eddie leaned down to lift the lid of the cistern and check the water supply. Almost every time, he would lose everything in his shirt pocket. When I finally had the cistern cleaned out, we found pens, receipts, and even a bucket on a rope.

That's where this next story comes in. In 2004, the pump for our cistern quit working. That meant when we turned on the water, it would either come out in a trickle, or if one of us happened to be taking a shower, it would blast that person up against the shower wall. My daughters were teenagers at the time, so it was miserable not having functioning water. For the next three days, we dipped water out of the cistern by tying a bucket on the end of a rope—that is, until the rope broke! While Eddie worked on replacing the pump, Rachel went to her friend's to get a shower. I was starting to turn into a dirty old lady, so I went with Mandy to my son's. I could almost smell the wonderful scent of water when we pulled up to his house.

When Eddie finally did get the new pump working, the basement kept flooding every time the pump came on. Then Eddie figured out he had the outside hose turned on full blast. So every time the pump came on, the hose was spraying water at the house, the ground was getting saturated, and the water was coming up through the basement. After he figured out that puzzle, he thought everything would be fine. But then our washer kept filling up with water until it overflowed. So we had to go to the Laundromat until we got it fixed. We felt like we were on *Survivor*, except we weren't going to win anything and we couldn't leave!

At times, moles would become a problem in our yard. Eddie was always wanting to reduce their population. One day I got home from work, and he was very excited. He said, "I got one, I got one, I got one!"

"You got what?" I asked.

"A mole." He went on to say that he saw one coming up out of a hole and he hit it over the head with shovel. He seemed so proud of his accomplishment that I half expected to see a flat-headed mole mounted over our fireplace.

***

In 1993, Eddie made a glider swing for us. One afternoon my daughters and I were sitting in it when suddenly the top boards came loose and the whole thing collapsed. Rachel screamed the most, even though she was the only one not hurt. Because of the way the glider fell, I ended up sitting on my leg so I could not get free. Mandy had one of the boards hit her head as the top fell in. Eddie was in the house watching TV, but it took him awhile to respond to our screams. When he finally came outside, I asked him what took him so long. He said he thought they were snake screams he was hearing, not hurt screams. I must admit—these screams did sound like the ones we made when we saw the occasional snake in our yard.

Uniquely Eddie

Over the years, I could always keep my friends and family entertained by telling them the latest stories about Eddie.

One time Eddie got me a peach tree for Mother's Day. He went outside to plant it. I watched as he dug a hole, scratched his head, moved over a bit, and started digging another hole.

"Why are you digging two holes for the same tree?" I asked.

He answered, "The first one wasn't big enough."

***

One year, when it was almost Christmas, I asked Eddie if he would go get me the Christmas tree that was on sale during a crazy Black Friday sale (more like Black-and-Blue Friday). I was surprised when he agreed to go, especially since he hated crowds. Maybe he thought that was his only chance to be surrounded by a bunch of screaming women. Anyway, I got my tree.

Eddie had a man cave in the basement, right under our bedroom, where he had his computer. He liked to play games where there were armies and guns involved. Of course, he had to turn the volume up high to get the full effect of the game. It was so loud that I could feel the bed shake, and the furniture seemed to want to rearrange itself. I felt like I was fighting a war right with them!

***

How common is it for someone to get painted into their garage? Get ready for an Eddie exclusive! He painted the house over the weekend one summer, and he painted it so well that the garage door was sealed shut. When I got up that Monday morning to go to work, I could not get the garage door open to get my car out. My garage was under my house, and I had the kids (who were small at time) in the car ready to leave for the babysitter's and for work. I called Eddie at work, and he told me what tools to get out of the barn to help with the door. Unfortunately, he remembered he had the only key.

I unsuccessfully tried to break free using a butter knife around the edges of the door. I then called my supervisor and told him he could send someone to get me out or I was going to have to take a vacation day. (My work was only ten minutes from home at the time.) My supervisor said that this was the best excuse he had ever heard for not coming to work on a Monday morning. He did end up coming to my house, and between the two of us, we were able to break the door free. After I finally got to work, one of my coworkers asked me if I left the car running while I was trying to get the garage door open. I told him, "No, that would have been *exhausting*!"

Maybe I should have just kept Eddie away from paint. I don't know why, but when he painted, he tended to paint around things rather than remove them. One such item was our wall phone in the living room. I guess he thought the phone would last forever, and we would never need to paint that room again. Of course, that wasn't the case. When the phone died, I had to put a wall hanging in its place until the room was repainted.

***

Eddie always appeared to stay calm no matter what the circumstances were. He was working as a welder when I had to call him at work on one particular occasion. After a few minutes of talking, he said, "Well, I really got to go now."

I said, "Oh, I know. You're at work, and I'm sure you're busy."

He replied, "No, it's not that. I just set my apron on fire."

Now I don't know about most people, but if I had just set myself on fire, panic would have been heard in my voice. It wasn't like that with Eddie. Of course, I hung up so he could put himself out.

Our routine in the morning was he would get up, get ready for work, and then wake me up. One morning I got up and he wasn't ready for work yet. I said, "Eddie, aren't you going to work today?"

He very calmly said, "No, I've been having chest pains for the last few days, so I am driving myself to the emergency room. But you go on to work and have a nice day."

Oh yeah, like that's going to happen. As it turned out, the chest pains were caused by stress (possibly from having set his apron on fire the week before?).

***

When our girls were small, Eddie and I took them to Kings Island Amusement Park. I took their wagon to pull them in. Believe it or not, Eddie was the first one to say he was tired and he wanted to go home. I was surprised he didn't ask the girls to get out of the wagon so I could let him ride for a while!

One time I noticed Eddie was staring at our cat for a very long time. He just kept looking at it. Finally I asked, "Eddie, why are you staring at the cat like that?" And he said, "Cat scan!"

As young children, my daughters would constantly want my help in finding misplaced items. Finally, after hearing my frustration, Eddie told the girls, "Look, you are going to have to keep up with your own things. It is not your mother's responsibility to keep track of everything." I was so happy someone was at last sympathetic to my problem. Not two minutes after that conversation ended, Eddie came to me and asked, "Hey, Sharon. Have you seen that screwdriver I was using last week? I seem to have misplaced it." Maybe his own rules didn't apply to husbands.

During my marriage to Eddie, I could never balance my checkbook. It wasn't all my fault, though. Eddie was very bad at telling me when he wrote a check and the amount of it. I thought I would solve that problem and get carbon checks, but that didn't help. He would just tear the check out of the book before he wrote it. I got used to never balancing my checkbook, which is a practice I still follow today. After all, isn't it the bank's job to know how much money I have?

I think the reason there are so many injuries in the home is because of husbands. For example, Eddie had a habit of pouring a glass of pop from a two-liter bottle but leaving the last two drops in the bottle. Instead of dumping it or just leaving the bottle out, he would put it back in the refrigerator with a thousandth of a millimeter of liquid left. Then some unsuspecting soul would come along (like me), open the refrigerator, and grab that two-liter bottle. My arm would swing back from the lack of weight, and I would just hope no one was standing behind me. I'm not one for wasting food, but if it prevents me from dislocating my shoulder, then I say dump the two remaining drops of pop down the drain!

One afternoon I used the drive-through at McDonald's. My van had electric windows, so I drove up, put my window down, and got my food. But then I couldn't get the window to go back up. On my way home, it started to rain—the first we'd had in weeks. When I got home, I parked in the garage. We ate our dinner, and Eddie said he was going to try to fix my window. His plan was to somehow pull it up because the mechanism was not working. Well, he was down in the garage for a little while, and then he came into the house and said, "You don't have to worry about that window anymore." I asked him why, and he said, "Because I broke it." The window had shattered inside the door as he was trying to pull up the glass. So to temporarily fix the problem, Eddie put plastic in the window's place and secured it with duct tape. It worked, but the noise it made when driving the van was almost enough to break my eardrums.

When our daughter, Mandy, was looking for her first car, Eddie was excited to tell her he found one. He came home with a tan 1986 Ford Escort that he paid seventy-five dollars for. It was two years older than Mandy was. She called it a "grandpa-mobile." Eddie was definitely happier finding the car than Mandy was getting it. But it got her where she needed to go.

***

Eddie and I stopped at McDonald's late one night, and I told him I'd wait out in the car while he went in to get our food. He said he would leave the car running since it was so cold outside. As he got out of our vehicle, he told me to lock the doors. "Oh," I said "no one would want an old lady like me."

"No," he replied, "but someone might want the car."

***

I came home from work one evening to a box of candy on the kitchen counter. I asked, "Eddie, who is this candy for?"

He said, "Well, it's for you."

"Why, is it Sweetest Day or something?" I started to panic because if it was, I didn't have anything for him.

But he answered, "I don't think so, but whatever holiday comes up next, I'm covered."

***

Eddie and I decided to go to the drive-in one summer evening. It was our first time there, and we weren't exactly sure it was. As we drove, we kept an eye out for it. Suddenly a business on the opposite side of the street caught our attention and in just that moment, we passed the drive-in. We didn't realize it until we were at the next small town, so we had to turn around and go back. What a pair we were.

***

When Eddie was in charge of dinner, we never knew what to expect. Once he went out for some fried chicken. It took him a long time to get home, even though the place was only about fifteen minutes away. When he finally returned, I noticed that he had the bucket of chicken, a broken window in his truck, and what looked like a new hammer in his hand. I said, "Eddie, I was getting worried. What took you so long?"

"Well," he began, "after I got the chicken, I realized I locked my keys in my truck. So I walked next door to the hardware store, bought a hammer, and knocked out the window."

"Eddie, why didn't you call me? I was home, and I had the extra key."

And he said, "I didn't want the chicken to get cold."

I had to wonder what the people in the hardware store thought. I mean, here was a guy going through the checkout line buying a hammer with a bucket of chicken under his arm. Did they think maybe the chicken wasn't quite dead yet?

***

One day I found my favorite pan in the sink and burnt beyond recognition. I immediately asked the kids if they did it, and they said no, it must have been their dad. When I asked Eddie about it, he admitted he was the guilty party. He said he had been making soup and fell asleep in the chair.

"Was it the smoke detector that woke you up?" I asked.

"No," he said. "I had to use the bathroom."

***

Another time I had just arrived home with the kids when we heard the smoke alarm going off as we pulled into the garage. Eddie was home making dinner. When I got upstairs, I saw flames coming out of a pot on my stove and Eddie asleep in the chair in the living room not twenty feet away. Apparently, he had been boiling potatoes, and all the water boiled away in the pot.

I don't know how he slept through all the noise. Obviously, he was not alarmed by it. I was the one who woke him up. He didn't seem surprised with all the commotion. He calmly walked over to the stove and put out the fire. He got upset with me for being upset with him for setting my stove on fire! It just wasn't my idea of a hot time. Thank goodness the only damage was a burned-up pot. I wouldn't recommend blackened potatoes—they really aren't good.

***

Eddie cooked a delicious spaghetti dinner for us one night. He had even stopped at the store to get some salad dressing for our salads. I had seen him shake up the dressing, but when it came time to use it, it was nowhere to be found. We looked and looked, and finally we went ahead and ate our spaghetti without the salads. My daughter came into the living room from the kitchen later that night and said she had found the salad dressing. She was holding an oven mitt. Apparently, Eddie had put the dressing on the edge of the island in the kitchen, and the bottle fell into the mitt that was hanging on the side of the island. What a scary household!

Eddie tried to make fudge one time, but something wasn't quite right. It never set up. We had it on top of the refrigerator for days, but it had the same nonfudge consistency the last day as it did the first. We finally declared it a failure. I'm not any better at that task. One time I tried to make divinity fudge that I could not get out of the bowl. I could pick up the bowl by the spoon I had in it.

When the kids and I arrived home one afternoon I saw Eddie making what appeared to be fried chicken. As I passed by the stove, I commented on how strangely cut the pieces of chicken were. He said, "Yeah, you know how our store is." I thought nothing more of it. A little while later, we sat down and ate dinner. Afterward, Eddie asked us how we liked the chicken. The children and I all said it was very good. Then he confessed: That wasn't chicken. It was rabbit. The kids freaked out when they realized they had eaten Thumper. But we did learn something—a lot of things *do* taste like chicken!

I turned on the oven one day and started to smell something burning as it got hot. When I looked inside, I found a cast-iron skillet covered in some kind of batter. Eddie had failed to tell me that he had been making cornbread in the skillet and spilled it. So he just left it in the oven for me to find (or smell). Maybe I should have just kept him out of the kitchen.

***

Sometimes wives say their husbands don't listen to them. I can tell you, on this occasion, Eddie did exactly what I asked him to do. I bought a roast for dinner, and I asked Eddie to put it in the Crock-Pot on low while I was at work. And that's exactly what he did. Unfortunately, I didn't ask him to plug in the Crock-Pot.

We were at Eddie's parents' for Thanksgiving one year, along with his brother. After dinner, the TV was turned on, which meant football was being watched. After a little while, both Eddie and his brother dozed off on the couch. My girls and I had had enough of football, so Rachel asked in a very low voice, "Mom, is it OK if I change the channel?" You would have thought she yelled it. Both of those guys were instantly awake. Proof that guys *do* listen.

****

When families go on vacation, they are usually looking for a little rest and relaxation. I'm not sure we got that with Eddie.

Our first camping trip with the kids was in 1998 and we had a very small car. After some maneuvering, we got everything packed without forgetting anything—like the kids, or worse yet, my nerve pills. The car was packed full with our tent and all the other gear that you need for such an outing. We couldn't have gotten another thing in if our lives depended on it. Amazingly, we were even more tightly packed on the way home, and we had to leave our dishpans behind. The obvious question is, *Why?* The answer is simple. I sent Eddie to the little campground store to get some hamburger buns, and he came back with an extra item—a TV. We were only camping for the weekend—in a tent, no less—but I guess he felt it was a necessity. And what kind of a camping store has hamburger buns, marshmallows, and oh yeah, TVs? It was a small one, just big enough to mess up packing the car for the return trip home. Several months after this trip, we traded the little car in for a van. At the car dealer's, we were cleaning it out, and there was an ax under the front seat. I hoped it was from the camping trip and Eddie didn't have a secret he wasn't telling me!

***

The following year, we took the kids camping again. It was the second time we used our tent. To make setting up easier, I had grouped, labeled, and taped the poles together. The first thing Eddie did when we arrived at the campsite was untape everything and put it in one big pile. That did not make me happy. It took a long while to get all the poles in the right place so our tent wouldn't look deformed. Also, Eddie tried to get our propane stove working while using a screwdriver on it and smoking a cigarette. That was a little scary.

One of our destinations on that trip was Put-In-Bay, Ohio. We rented one of those electric cars, but neither Eddie nor I could figure out how to start it. Finally a nine-year-old boy showed us how. Thank goodness for kids. Then our van got a flat tire on the way home while we were on the highway. We had to pull over to the shoulder while Eddie changed it. He ended up unloading half our stuff for nothing—he was looking in the wrong place for the spare tire. Besides that, after we got home, we discovered he had left half our jack on the side of the highway. We should never have been allowed on the road without adult supervision.

***

One year Eddie and I flew to Las Vegas with my sister. We were standing in front of Treasure Island watching the show they put on when my sister asked me to use her camera to take a video of her in front of the casino. After I took the video, I held the camera down to my side as we waited for my sister to return. As we waited, I mentioned to Eddie that I wished she would venture out on her own more so we could spend more time alone. Just about that time, my sister came back, took her camera, and said, "Hey, you didn't turn the camera off." I panicked. I thought for sure the conversation I just had with Eddie would be on there. A few weeks after we returned home she asked me to come over to her house and see the video of the trip. What could I do? I couldn't get out of it. I agreed, but I held my breath as the video played. Thank goodness, apparently there was too much other noise for my conversation to be picked up. For once luck was on my side.

In 2004, Eddie and I went to Virginia for a few days. We stayed in a little cabin near a lake, and the scenery was beautiful. On our last morning there, we went out on the deck to drink our coffee, and I closed the cabin door behind us. Eddie asked if I had locked us out. I was sure I didn't. But I was wrong. Since Eddie was not able, I knew I would have to walk up to the lodge to get help. I wasn't looking forward to this. I had just woken up, and besides not wearing a bra, my hair was standing on end. Eddie gave me the jacket he was wearing, and I began making my way to the lodge, which was about a fifteen-minute walk from our cabin. Fortunately, I found a cabin on the way that had lights on inside. I knocked on the door, and the family there allowed me to use their phone to call the lodge. By the time I made it back, Eddie had already picked the lock with his driver's license, a talent I didn't know he had. He got in faster than the security guy could get there.

***

In 2005, Eddie and I went to Aruba, along with my son and his wife. The stories begin right at the airport as we were trying to leave Cincinnati. We didn't need passports, but we did need our original birth certificates and our driver's licenses. We got up to the counter, and I gave them what I thought was Eddie's birth certificate, since it had the pretty gold seal on it. The guy behind the counter looked at it and told me it wouldn't work. It was from the hospital, not the state. I panicked. I didn't want to leave Eddie behind, but I was prepared to do so if necessary. I really wanted to go to Aruba. As it turned out, Eddie had a credit card-looking thing that his mom had gotten for him years ago and it had all the pertinent information on it. That was exactly what was needed. Eddie was relieved that he would see Aruba in person and not just in my pictures.

We had a wonderful time in Aruba. A few days into our trip, we were returning to our hotel from a snorkeling trip. We were being driven back by one of the operators of the boat we were just on, and he was telling us a little bit about himself. The language in Aruba is a little bit of English and a little bit of something else. The guy said he liked his job on the boat, but he had another job he liked even better. I asked him what that was, and he said "I train ducks."

I repeated, "You train ducks?"

"Yes, I train ducks."

I thought this was so cool. "What do you train them to do?" I asked.

"Oh, all kinds of things," he said. "They help the police, and I even do behavioral training when they misbehave for their owners."

After getting the image in my mind of ducks going on drug raids for the police and hiding the evidence under their little wings, I realized he was really saying that he trained *dogs*! My family and I laughed about that one for the rest of the trip.

Several days into our vacation, I woke up with a huge bottom lip. It felt so big I was afraid to look in the mirror. After seeing chicken feet in the grocery store there, I thought someone might have put a voodoo curse on me or something. It felt so weird. I was afraid I would drool when I ate; it felt the same way as when I got novocaine from the dentist. It turned out sunburned lips were the problem.

On our trip home, the flight made a stop in New York. We only had forty minutes to get our luggage and board the next plane. After waiting as long as we could, we finally had to continue on without our bags. We were told they would be found and brought to us. But of course the truck bringing it the next day ran out of gas on the side of the road, and we didn't get our luggage until that night.

Sadly this was the last vacation for me and Eddie. He died in March the following year.

Gordy

I never thought I would get married again, but God had other plans for me. In early 2009, Elizabeth, a friend from church, called me and asked if I would like to meet her brother.

My reply was, "Yes, but if he is looking for a wife, I am not looking for a husband."

Elizabeth told me to come to her mom's house on that Saturday to meet Gordy. The plan was to have pizza delivered and we would play cards. So on that Saturday, I headed over to my destination, which was only a few streets from me. When I saw a pizza delivery being made at the front door, I pulled into the driveway. Except that I was at the house next door. Apparently, pizza was in demand that night.

But I made it to the right house, where I met Gordy. I thought he was cute immediately, but he was so quiet. We played cards, and I left not knowing what he thought of me, especially when he let me walk out into the dark to my car alone. But he called me the next day, and we continued to see each other.

Being a little cautious, however, I did not tell Gordy where I lived at first. I would meet him with my own car when we made our dates. After all, as I told Gordy, "Even serial killers have moms who love them." I was not taking any chances. So we drove separately for several months until I decided Gordy was not dangerous after all and I could trust him. That's when I showed him where I lived and introduced him to "Cape Fear," as we began calling my house at that time.

I introduced Gordy to my two dogs and three cats, which was a bit scary. I had been told he was not the animal lover I am. He was no dog whisperer by any means. In fact, he was a dog yeller, and I even called him Old Yeller. But over time, my pets knew how to act when Gordy was around. Mostly, they would run and hide. He was never mean to them, but animals have a way of knowing if you like them or not. When Cape Fear and the animals didn't scare him off, I knew our relationship had possibilities. Gordy and I continued to date and enjoy each other's company.

On one of our dates, Gordy and I went to a movie. It was winter, and our part of theater was extremely cold. It was almost warmer outside than where we were. The heating system was not working for that particular theater—everywhere else in the building was nice and toasty.

After the movie, we decided to stop at a restaurant and get dessert and coffee. I kept my eye out for available restaurants, but Gordy kept passing them up as fast as I was pointing them out. After missing several turns, we ended up at Max & Erma's. We looked at the menu for several minutes, trying to decide what dessert to get. The waiter suggested the banana cream pie. He went on and on about how good it was and how we must try it. So we told him he talked us into it—we would definitely get the banana cream pie. We couldn't wait to try it since he bragged on it so much. To our disappointment, however, the waiter returned a few minutes later to tell us that they were out of banana cream pie. Not only that, but we never got spoons for our coffee. I hoped my bad luck was not infecting Gordy!

It seemed that my bad luck stuck only to me, though. One time while dating, I made a pie and brought it to Gordy's house. I had it on a pie plate with a lid. Somehow I lost my grip on it as I was going up the front steps. The lid to the container came off, the pie flipped, and it landed on the pie plate upside down. Surprisingly, the pie never hit the ground.

I had gall bladder surgery in May 2009, and I stayed at Gordy's mom's during my recovery. Gordy was there most of the time as well. He would stop by my house and take care of my cats and dogs and then check on his own home, which was a forty-five-minute drive from mine. On one of these trips back to his house, he discovered his electric had gone out sometime that week. He said when he walked in the house, the smell was horrible. Everything in his refrigerator and freezer had gone bad. After cleaning all that up and coming back to his mom's, we went out for dinner. We were waiting for our food when we heard a loud crash. The waitress came over to our table and asked if we heard the commotion. That was Gordy's dinner. They had to make him a new steak. Then on the way home, a tree had fallen in the middle of the road. We had to wait until it cleared. This all happened the same day. The previous day, Gordy had gotten a flat tire while coming to pick me up. I was beginning to think my luck is his luck after all.

In October 2009, Gordy and I went to see the replica of Christopher Columbus's ships, which were docked on the Kentucky side of the Ohio River. Afterward, we ate at a restaurant called Buckheads, where Gordy managed to squirt catsup in the air when he thought the bottle was empty. Later we went to Newport on the Levee and walked around some more, since it was such a beautiful day. We got ice cream at the Stone Cold Creamery there. Somehow I managed to tip my cup of ice cream, and I got it all over my pants.

When the *Lost Egypt* exhibit came to Cincinnati in the fall of 2009, Gordy and I decided to go. It was a very interesting exhibit, but the experience was not without incident. Gordy was chewing gum, not knowing it was not allowed. One of the volunteers approached him and asked, "Is that gum?" With that, she followed him around with a little trash can until he spit it out. Maybe she thought he was a big student with one of the school groups that were there. But what about all his facial hair? He would have had to be a student with a very bad hormone problem. He told me later that he should have said the gum was an artifact.

Around this same time, Gordy helped me take the middle seat out of my van. I needed to get my lawn mower in to take it to the repair shop. We set the seat to one side of the garage, and I was very careful when I drove the van in not to get too close to it. That worked for a while. One fateful day, however, I got a call on my cell phone about Mandy's riding helmet, which I had listed on Craigslist. I had to get home before the potential buyer got there. In my rush, when I pulled into my garage, I got too close to the van seat. I ran into the metal piece sticking out of the bottom with my front tire. The next thing I knew, I heard a *pop, pop, pop,* and my tire went flat instantly. I didn't encounter a road hazard—I encountered a garage hazard. I quickly put the van in reverse and backed out of the garage so I wouldn't be stuck there. There was no fixing the tire; it had a huge slit in it. My son came to my house and put on my spare mini tire. Thanks to Craigslist, I had just sold Mandy's bed and the riding helmet, but by the time I paid for the new tire, I made a huge profit of five dollars.

***

Before Gordy gave me my real engagement ring, he gave me one to hold its place. Of course, this ring wasn't as beautiful as the one I got later, but I still loved it for what it meant. One day I was raking leaves in my yard and then burning them. In the process, I lost that first ring. I knew it was lost somewhere in the pile of burning leaves. After looking for it without success, I gave up. When I told my daughter, Mandy, about it, she said maybe it was a sign that Gordy and I shouldn't get married. I told her that wasn't true. It was really a sign of our hot, burning love. Happily, Gordy brought over his metal detector, and we were able to find my "ring of fire."

When Gordy later presented me with a beautiful engagement ring, of course I was eager to show it off. We were at a dance sitting with another couple who are friends of ours. The woman wanted to see the ring, and I was impressed when she put on her sunglasses to look at it. Was it really sparkling too brightly to look at with the naked eye? I began to laugh, and she told me that those were prescription sunglasses. Well, the ring is still gorgeous.

Gordy and I got married in 2010. I tell people I come from a long line of Hookers, and it took me fifty-five years to get a Hickey. It's true. My mother's maiden name was Hooker, and I was fifty-five when I married Gordy.

We had a rehearsal the day before our wedding, and then a few of us went to a little restaurant in our neighborhood. My son was telling us how Bruno, their dog, bit into my grandson Adam's tetherball and deflated it. Gordy asked Adam if Bruno was still busting his balls. Gordy really wished he had rephrased his question.

Our wedding took place at our church. I was so nervous I told my friends I didn't need a flower girl. I would be shaking my flowers all the way down the aisle and leave petals everywhere.

Gordy and I went to Fort Myers, Florida, for our honeymoon. As usual my bad luck was with us. My luggage was damaged during our flight—no surprise there. It had wheels, but they seemed flat as I was trying to drag it through the airport to our taxi. It was storming badly in Florida, which made the chore even more unpleasant.

We were absolutely soaked by the time we got to our hotel. We were a little early, and we were told our room was not quite ready. So we walked around Fort Myers for a little while. It was still raining, and even the locals were commenting on how unusual it was to get this much rain. When we checked on the room once more, I couldn't believe it. It still wasn't ready. Gordy and I just wanted to be able to get out of our wet clothes. Then we observed other people coming in after us and getting their rooms. That's when I lost it and almost went postal at the front desk. Needless to say, a few minutes later, we finally got access to our room. Gordy said he saw a side of me he had never seen before.

***

As I mentioned, early in our relationship, Gordy and I referred to my house as "Cape Fear," which is where we planned to live. At times I would dream of my house being taken out by some unforeseen event. Where was that out-of-control bulldozer when I needed it? I always thought if I won the lottery, I would rent a bulldozer and take out the house myself. Why couldn't my little town decide to put a bypass right through my living room? At one point, I had a very bad water problem in my basement. Even if it rained lightly, I would end up with a flood. One time I even found a dragonfly living down there. I felt sorry for all the homeless fish and frogs when I finally got the basement waterproofed. Before I met Gordy, I almost wanted to call the place whose advertisement reads, "We Buy Ugly Houses." But what if my house was even too ugly for them? That would be the ultimate rejection. Would I be referred to a support group?

Shortly after we were married, Gordy began remodeling my kitchen, which was a much-needed project. It was almost too depressing to eat in there. For one thing, it was painted a bad color green which I liked to call "gangrene." Eddie had found that paint in the discontinued discount aisle of the hardware store, and now we know why. The kitchen was so dark it was like eating in a cave. Gordy and I decided to change the green to a nice, cheerful yellow. But when Gordy began painting, it was like two worlds were colliding. The old rejected the new, and bubbles began to appear. He had to repaint the walls several times before the yellow paint won.

The nightmares at Cape Fear are not over yet. Gordy thought he was done with the gangrene paint until I told him it was also used in the second bathroom. That little room was off limits to him for a long time. We were married over a year before I got the nerve to show it to him. That project is yet to be tackled.

Another improvement was the barn makeover. The once-red paint had faded, and the barn had turned pink. After a new paint job and new doors, it looks like a guy's place again. As the improvements began to happen, we changed the name for the house from Cape Fear to Cape Hope. Maybe I'll put a hold on that bulldozer for now.

***

We have a lot of trees around our house, so there is continual yard work. One fall I told Gordy I was SOL—Sick of Leaves. It seemed like they were never-ending. I accused him of taking leaves from our neighbor's yard and putting them in ours.

A few years ago, Gordy got an idea that we should put an ice skating rink in our yard. It does get cold enough in the winter to freeze a rink, and it would be fun for my grandchildren and the kids at our church. So we started buying up skates we found in thrift stores or being sold online. I told Gordy I am always on the lookout for some "cheap skates."

Several years ago, we had a family of raccoons living in our barn. I didn't see them, but Gordy said there were babies and at least one mom. We had a very long extension cord we kept in the barn for the sole purpose of being able to use our weed eater all over the yard. One day we couldn't find the extension cord anywhere, and the raccoons had also suddenly disappeared. Was there a connection?

***

In May 2011, Gordy and I went to Las Vegas. One of the days there was very cold, windy, and rainy. They only get five inches of rain a year, and it had to happen when we were there.

On this same trip, we stopped at the nearby store to get some food to take back to our hotel. We were in the breakfast aisle, where I saw Gordy reach down to the bottom shelf and grab the chocolate cereal. I teased him about it because in my mind, only a child would want that cereal. I guess I gave him a complex, because he put it back. When we got back from our trip, I took an unscientific survey of my friends, and the consensus was if we were on vacation, he should have been able to get any kind of cereal he wanted. So I have changed my view on that. In fact, recently I announced very loudly while we were in the grocery store that I found his chocolate cereal. I didn't mean to be that loud, but I was not very close to Gordy when I spotted it. I wanted him to know he could quit looking for it. I think the other adults in the aisle thought it was funny. Maybe they secretly wanted chocolate cereal too.

***

In July 2014, Gordy and I flew to Fort Myers, Florida, for a week of sun and relaxation. On the flight there, we had a female pilot and copilot, which I thought was great. After all, if we got lost, at least they would ask directions!

24

Once there, we definitely got the sun, but I'm not sure about the relaxation. My friend, Debi, and her husband, Steve, live in Cape Coral, which is not far from Fort Myers. They graciously offered to pick us up from the airport and take us to the little cottage we had rented. After arriving at the airport, I received a call on my cell phone from Debi asking me which airline we had taken. By no fault of their own, they went to the wrong airport about thirty miles from where we were at Punta Gorda. After picking us up, they drove us to the grocery store to get a few food items to take to the cottage. One of those items was a watermelon—a thirty-three-pound one. In an attempt to cut it later that evening, I dropped half of it on the floor! What a mess!

A day or two later, Gordy and I went to a little cafe for lunch. One of the specials of the day was a fish sandwich. I asked the waitress what kind of fish it was, and she said it was haddock. I asked Gordy if that would be something I would like, since I don't like fishy-tasting fish. He said I would, and I told the waitress that was what I wanted. When we got our food, I was presented with two small hamburgers. I told the waitress that was not what I ordered and she insisted that it was. Proof that I can have a bad restaurant experience no matter what state I'm in.

About the third day of our vacation, Gordy and I were getting ready to leave the cottage to go down to the beach. He was a little red from the sun, and he was applying some cream on his legs. I asked him what he was doing, and he said he was putting on sunscreen. I told him that wasn't sunscreen; it was the hand lotion for my dry skin. He told me that was what he used for the last two days.

We went down to the beach, rented two chairs and an umbrella, and spent most of the day there. As luck would have it, we sat near an Elvis impersonator—a very bad one. The likeness stopped at the hair. He mostly looked and sounded like a comedian I remembered seeing on TV, even when he "sang" at the request of the beach disc jockey. I wanted to request he quit singing! I hope he didn't quit his day job.

When we returned to the cottage, Gordy's legs, especially his ankles, were very, very red. He ended up with a severe sunburn, which made the rest of the trip not-so relaxing for him. I always knew he was hot, but now he was really hot! Apparently, the hand lotion he had applied by accident for three days was not sunscreen, but sun *scream*.

A few days later, I got a medical condition of my own. I woke up with a huge bottom lip, probably caused by the sun and wind. Between Gordy's burnt legs and my big lip, we were quite a couple. I felt like we were given our own section of the restaurant whenever we went out to eat.

On our return trip home, our flight was delayed. We were told there were mechanical problems, so we had a three-hour wait until another plane could be flown in from Saint Petersburg. When I received the text on my phone from the airline informing us of this information, I decided to keep my friend, Debi, updated as to what was happening. After finishing my text to her and trying to send it, I got a second communication asking me if I really wanted to send that message. There might be a charge, I was informed. That was when I realized what I had almost done: instead of sending Debi a text, I was responding to the airline. Oops.

Gordy and I thought that would be the end of our stories for this trip, but there was one more. Shortly into our flight home, there was a medical emergency, and thank goodness, there were doctors on board to deal with that situation. When I texted my daughter letting her know about it, she assumed I was the reason for the emergency. (She really knows her mother.) She was quite relieved when I told her otherwise.

***

Our county fair was in July 2014, and Gordy and I went to watch the demolition derby. Extra stands were brought in to handle the crowd, and we were sitting in the top row, which had slats in the back. I was just sitting there enjoying the entertainment when I heard a clunk and felt something hit my neck. I figured it was a rock. I turned around and caught a glimpse of someone running. A lady and her child happened to be standing below, and she shouted that she had just witnessed a boy flinging a Blow Pop up into the stands. As my luck would have it, I was the one who was hit. The police who were monitoring the crowd then began their search for this kid. I don't know if they found him or not. I'm guessing the charge would be assault with a deadly lollipop.

A few years ago, Gordy and I visited New York. We saw a lady who was traveling and had a little dog in a pet carrier bag. I think it was a New Yorkie.

On our second anniversary, we enjoyed a nice dinner and then went to see *The Three Stooges*. Normal people may think this is a weird movie choice for this occasion, but who said we were normal?

***

Gordy and I both love our treats. One of Gordy's favorite desserts is my homemade cheesecake. After dinner one evening, he said, "I think I'm going to get a piece of that cheesecake."

I replied, "Uh, no you won't. I had the last of it this afternoon."

"Oh," he said, "then I will have some potato chips."

Again I said, "No, you won't. I finished off those too." Poor Gordy.

***

When Gordy went back to work after the Thanksgiving holiday, he had my kind of luck. First he stopped at two ATMs to withdraw some money. They were both out. Later that day his coworker came up to him and said, "You are wearing blue underwear, aren't you?" Within seconds Gordy realized he had somehow caught his pants on the machine he was running and ripped the butt out of them. But he got resourceful and made the best of the situation. When it was time for Gordy to come home, our vehicle wouldn't shift, so he was stuck until I picked him up. That's when I learned how he had fixed his pants problem: duct tape! It's true that it can fix anything.

Gordy and I are both electronically challenged. Every time we get a new device, we need help. Mandy got our new printer set up. I did learn how to text on my own, but the first time I did it, I scared my kids. They called to make sure my phone wasn't stolen and that it was actually me using it. I got Gordy a tablet one Christmas and was trying to set it up. Somehow I managed to set it to German instead of English. Mandy was living with us at the time, and she told us we were not allowed to get any more electronics until after she moved out. That would solve her problem, but what about ours? I think Gordy and I need adult supervision.

We got a new computer in 2012 when our old desktop got extremely slow. It was nice to have one that was so fast we didn't need a calendar to measure its speed.

On Christmas Day 2013, I visited my family early in the day. The plan was to go to Gordy's sister's that evening for the family gathering. The time was changed several times, but the last we heard, it was still on for the evening. We got there, and surprise, surprise, no one else was around! We found out the gathering had been held earlier in the day, but we had not been informed about the latest change in time. Everyone assumed we were busy with my family, so no one called to find out where we were. We were all dressed up with no place to go.

Never let a smoker who hates winter try to quit during a polar vortex. It's not pleasant. More than once Gordy thought about buying cigarettes, and more than once I was going to let him. But I am pleased to say Gordy has been smoke-free since January 2014.

***

Gordy has several interesting hobbies. One is sailing. Several years ago, we purchased a small sailboat. In order to get the trailer licensed, we had to get it weighed. So we connected the boat and trailer to the hitch on our van and headed for the lake. The plan was to put the boat in the lake, and then Gordy was going to hold it in place by the ropes while I drove the trailer to the weigh station. It sounded like a simple plan.

Here's what happened. The hitch came off our van when we were about one minute from our house. The boat and trailer were stuck in the middle of the road. We had to manually pull them off the street and leave them in a stranger's yard. We explained our dilemma to the homeowner, and we had to leave the boat there for several hours while we got the hitch reattached.

On our second try, the hitch didn't fall off, but we did struggle to get the boat in the water because of the angle of the ramp. After some maneuvering, we finally succeeded, and I left with the trailer to get it weighed. So here I was driving a van with a big trailer on the back, which I wasn't used to, and looking for the weigh station. Of course, it wasn't easy to find. I passed it more than once. After turning around several times, I finally found the place.

Eventually, I made it back to the lake. We got the boat loaded on the trailer and sat in the parked van for a moment before starting home. But that still isn't the end of the story. The van wouldn't start. After tinkering with it for a few minutes, Gordy got it started. And he said sailing was relaxing!

***

Gordy's other hobbies include winemaking and beekeeping. He wears a one-piece bee suit and hood whenever he needs to get into the hive to check its progress. I will never forget the double take he got when he was taking the trash to the curb while in his bee gear just about the time the garbage truck arrived.

We are also the proud owners of seven chickens. If someone wants to know about the birds and the bees, they can come to our house.

One of the things Gordy got to cross off his bucket list was owning a BMW. We recently purchased one that he had seen for sale on his way to work. Every time he drives it, he tells me how much he loves it. I told him that's fine, but if he starts looking under the hood of the car more than he looks under mine, he's going to be in trouble.

CHAPTER 2

THE THREE CHILDREN

I like to tell people I have three children—one of each. I get interesting looks—and my own space in a crowded elevator.

Fun-Loving Robert

My son Robert has always been a source of entertainment. With his natural sense of humor, he has always been a joy to be around.

When Robert was three, he started preschool. He was learning the parts of the body, and I was watching as he put them in place on the cardboard figure. When he was handed the nose, he didn't put it on the face, he put it down there. It *was* a funny looking nose. Both his teacher and I had to smile about that one.

I have saved some of the papers and artwork Robert made in school over the years. One was from when he was in preschool. Apparently, the children were looking for certain colors in magazines. The picture Robert chose for purple was a shapely young woman wearing a purple swimsuit. What kind of magazines were these children given? And what was my son thinking at age four?

When Robert was five, he found a cute way of letting us know his Christmas wish list. He cut pictures out of magazines and wrote yes on some of them and no on others. He then put all the pictures in an envelope addressed to

Santa and gave them to me. Not a bad idea for a kid. I knew exactly what he wanted and what he didn't want.

I found this note written to my son, but I don't remember who wrote it. I hope it wasn't me.

Dear Bobby,

Are you being a good boy? I hope so. I am giving you one of your surprises now if you are good. I will bring more surprises to you on Christmas Day.

Be a good boy, and remember I love you.

Santa Claus

PS: I know where you live, and I have a key to get in the door!

The first part of this note isn't bad, but that last sentence is just plain creepy.

Unlike his mother, Robert was always good at learning new things—and he still is. My niece is a year older than he is, and when she was trying to learn how to ride her bike, she just did not get the hang of it. Both of her parents tried unsuccessfully to teach her. They were at our house one day when Robert said he would help her. So he and my niece went down to our basement, and in a matter of minutes, he had her riding a bike. Problem solved!

I reserved a party room at McDonald's for Robert's sixth birthday party. I assumed it would be nice, but I was wrong. In fact, I had never seen a party room like this. To get to it, we were led through the kitchen, down some stairs, and into what appeared to be a sub-basement. From there it was like a going through a mouse maze getting around the pipes and the heating and cooling duct work until we got to our destination. I guess the fact that there was a giant Ronald McDonald in the corner technically made it a place to have a party, but I wouldn't call it a party room. Also, I think since we were out of sight, we were also out of mind. The service we got was not good. The only entertainment the kids had was climbing on the giant Ronald McDonald. It was a little top-heavy, and I was afraid we would have a McAccident.

When Robert was about six years old, we went camping in Brown County, Indiana. This area is known for having many deer. I was told that they were so tame you could walk right up to them and even feed them from your hand. We encountered a group of deer while driving to our campsite, and we got out of the car to see them. We must have come in contact with the only psychotic one in the herd, because this particular deer ran up to my son and kicked him to the ground, ripping his new jeans. This was definitely a deer with an attitude.

***

My son has liked some weird food combinations over the years. As a child, he enjoyed eating jelly and mayonnaise sandwiches from time to time. He also loved ketchup. He would carefully put his food on his plate in separate spots. Then he would add ketchup and stir everything together.

Maybe his tastes in food made him the funny guy he is today. When he was young, even in his teenage years, I would try to take a video of him, and he would stay perfectly still—not even blinking. Everyone around him would be moving, and he would be as motionless as a statue.

And he enjoys scaring family members. One time I got into my van and found a rubber snake draped over my steering wheel. It's not uncommon to be visiting with him and have a rubber mouse show up somewhere. Once he placed a scary Halloween mask on the end of a broom handle to frighten our dog. He ended up scaring me too, and I think both the dog and I both growled at him. He also likes to put tea lights in his eyes or pretend to smoke my battery-operated candles. And he likes to stick socks on his ears. He is quite entertaining to be around.

When Robert turned twenty in 1997, he had a strange birthday request. He wanted dog food. He had just got a little puppy he named Patch. I got him a twenty-pound bag of dog food, and my sister got him a wicker bowl full of doggie biscuits. I'm assuming all of it was for Patch.

Before my daughter-in-law married Robert, she had a cat named Hamilton. I was visiting at her apartment one day, and I commented on how gentle Hamilton was when he played with his toy I was holding. Vickie sort of laughed and then told me he was declawed. Sometimes I am a little slow catching on.

***

Robert got married in 2003. At the rehearsal dinner, there were about twenty or more of us sitting at a big long table. Dinner was uneventful until the waiter cleared the table. I heard him say "Whoops!" but I didn't know what happened until my daughter, Mandy, told me later. She said that one of the open pats of butter fell off one of the plates he was carrying, and it did a couple of flips before it landed on the back of my sweater. Of course, it just had to land butter-side down, which caused the thing to stick. The waiter then very gently reached over and picked it off my back without saying a word. I felt nothing.

At the wedding the next day, the minister was having Vickie repeat the wedding vows. He said, "I, Vickie, take Kevin …" Vickie responded well by putting Robert's name in place of Kevin's. Everyone started to laugh, and the minister was a bit embarrassed. He said he was just testing us to see if we were listening.

At the reception, one of Robert's friends introduced himself to me and asked who I was. I told him that I was Robert's mother. I also stated that I recognized him from the rehearsal and the dinner the night before. He said he did not remember seeing me there at all.

***

Robert has always been a very hard worker. He owns his own lawn care business. A few years ago, he was having stomach pains, so he made an appointment with the doctor but then canceled when the symptoms went away. The next thing we knew, he said he was going to the emergency room with Vickie after doing "one more lawn." It turns out he had to have an emergency appendectomy. Such dedication to his job.

One time he was on his way to cut a lawn when he witnessed a car being cut off. It lost control and went down an embankment. He said people were stopping to look, but no one was helping. He parked his truck, pulled the first lady out, and then pulled the second lady out. I asked him what he did when the police got there, and he said, "Mom, I didn't have time to wait for the police. I had lawns to cut."

***

In 2006, Robert and Vickie welcomed their son, Adam, into the world. When he was little, Adam thought that the name on the bottom of his socks was his, not Hanes. He learned a lot of things in preschool, and one day I asked him to spell his name. He said "B-I-N-G-O." When Adam was three, Gordy and I got him and his dad both an electronic guitar shirt that really played. When Adam put his on, he yelled, "Let's rock and roll!" In 2012, Gordy and I got Adam a pogo stick for Christmas, which he said he had been "wanting for years." He was six.

Adam likes to be just like his dad, so he is learning how to be a trickster too. While at my house during Christmas 2013, he hid in a big, empty box and waited for his mom and dad to "unwrap" him. Unfortunately, Robert and Vickie got distracted. It took them quite awhile to find him. All the while, Adam patiently waited.

One Easter, Robert and Adam were decorating eggs with the vinegar/water mix, and Robert pretended to drink the mixture. Adam did the same. It freaked me out!

Robert was working on his car one day, and Adam was right there with him. When they came in the house, they were both dirty in the same spots.

When I play cards with Adam, I am prepared for two sets of rules—one for Adam and one for me. And when he plays a board game or tic-tac-toe with me, I am careful not to turn my back on him!

Robert and Vickie found out they were going to be parents for the second time in 2011. Adam was hoping for a little brother. When he found out he was getting a sister instead, he just hung his head. The new addition was due in mid-August, and Gordy suggested Vickie wait until the twenty-third of the month so they could share the same birthday. Vickie had a better idea. She suggested Gordy change *his* birthday. Adam turned out to be a great big brother. In fact, he tried to feed his sister Cheerios before they even left the hospital.

In 2011, I decided to make Vickie a Christmas stocking. Robert had the one I had made when he was little, and I had already made one for Adam and new baby Emily. I got a kit and began cutting out the tiny pieces of felt that Vickie's stocking required. One evening I was in the living room, sitting on the couch and watching TV while I was doing the cutting. I dropped one of the tiny pieces, and somehow it disappeared down in between the couch cushions. It was really small, and I had a hard time finding it, but I did. Just after I retrieved it, however, I managed to drop it in a glass that was sitting on the coffee table that had a few drops of lemonade left in it. I basically had to wash that tiny piece of fabric before I could sew it onto the stocking. No experience is normal for me.

After Easter dinner in 2014, I asked everyone if they would like a piece of the cheesecake I made for dessert. Adam said he wanted the cake but didn't want the cheese.

Recently I discovered it was time to update the toys my grandchildren play with when they come to visit. When he found one of my house slippers, Adam asked Emily if she wanted to play toss the shoe. That was my sign.

***

My son and his family have a dog named Bruno. He is a big lab, and he is very sweet. When they go swimming in their backyard pool, Bruno is the first one in. In years past, he would let Adam hold on to his tail while he pulled him around the pool.

For Valentine's Day 2013, I made cupcakes and took them to my son's house for them to enjoy. I decorated them and even put the names of my son, daughter-in-law, granddaughter, and grandson on them. They put them on their kitchen counter and went out for a while. When they came back, there were no cupcakes. Only cupcake holders. Bruno had got them off the counter and enjoyed himself. Maybe he was upset because his name wasn't on one of them. One time he also ate my grandchild's macaroni art.

Chocolate-Seeking Rachel

There are plenty of amusing stories about my second child, Rachel.

When Rachel was a baby, she didn't just cry; she screamed—a lot. When she was about six months old, I took her to work on my vacation day to show her off. My office was on the eleventh floor. Rachel was not happy that day and, as we rode the elevator, she made that fact known all the way to our destination.

When Rachel was just learning to talk, she managed to say everyone's name clearly except mine. She called me Bo-bo.

***

A few weeks before she started kindergarten, I wanted to make sure Rachel knew the basics, such as her name, address, and telephone number. Of course, she knew her first and last name, but I wasn't sure she knew her middle name. "Rachel," I said, "Do you know your full name?"

"Yes, Mommy, I think I do," was her reply. "It's Rachel Little Darling Witherington."

"Little Darling?" I asked. "Why do you think that is your middle name?"

"Because," she said, "whenever I go to Grandma's, she says, 'There's Rachel, my little darling.'"

What could I say to that?

***

When Rachel was little, whenever she heard the oldies song "Down in the Boondocks," she would sing along to "Down in the Boom Box." Also, instead of "The Star Spangled Banner," Rachel thought it was "The Star

Bengal Banner." And instead of "twilight's last gleaming," for her it was "Bengals are sleeping." Some years, I think that's actually true.

When she was young, Peter Pan was Rachel's favorite movie. One time we had gone to watch Robert compete in a race with his remote control car at a little race track in Indiana. Rachel noticed a young man who had an artificial hand who happened to be another spectator. She couldn't keep this exciting discovery to herself, so she yelled in her loudest voice, "Look, Mom! It's Captain Hook!" What does a mom do in a case like that except apologize—and hide somewhere.

One time Rachel literally lost her tooth when it came out. She dropped it down the drain during a Girl Scout meeting. I had to convince her that the tooth fairy would not forget her, even though she didn't have the tooth.

When the kids were small and I took them trick-or-treating, Rachel had a bad habit of staring into the door of the house until someone answered. It was particularly scary one year when the cloth head of her ghost outfit was on sideways.

I could always tell if Rachel was telling a fib when she was little. She would stick out her tongue and start licking her lips.

Rachel was playing with some plastic darts that had suction cups on the ends. She thought it would be funny if she stuck one on her forehead. When she removed it, however, she discovered it left a big red mark. As luck would have it, she had a doctor's appointment that afternoon. The mark was still there several hours later when we had to leave for the doctor's office, so she combed her bangs down to cover it up. The doctor lifted up her bangs, saw the mark, and said, "Hey, I've never noticed that birthmark before."

Rachel came to me one day concerned about the dark spot on the back of her neck. After taking a look at it, I provided a cure: do a better job washing.

She was chewing gum in the car one day and decided to spit it out the window. When she did, the wind blew it back in the car, and it landed in her long hair. Is it possible she has my luck?

Sometimes as parents we help our kids too much, like when Rachel was young and she and I played Scrabble. My motherly guidance used to take over when she was struggling to make a play. Instead of allowing her to get six points on her own, I would show her a way to get twenty-seven points by using a triple word score square. And she would win. Basically I beat myself at the game. To make matters worse, Rachel would brag to everyone how she was a better player than her mother.

***

There wasn't much conflict between my son and my daughters. There was a nine-year difference between him and Rachel, and an eleven-year difference between him and Mandy, so they didn't have much to fight about. The girls, however, were a different story.

One time they were both in the backseat of the car when Rachel said, "Mom, will you make Mandy stop? She's bothering me."

"What is she doing?" I asked.

The reply was, "She's making me laugh, and I don't feel like being happy today." How do I solve a problem like that? Should I have made a rule that there will be no happy children that could cause unwanted laughter in the car?

***

Mornings can be hectic when you have children. Between getting them out the door to school and still getting to work on time yourself, it can be crazy. On one of these mornings, Mandy was frantically looking for her shoes with no success. I went into the living room to help her look when I saw Rachel stuffing Mandy's shoes under the couch. Busted!

Once when they were teenagers, I got a call at work from Rachel. She said, "Mom, if Mandy calls you and says I punched her out, I probably did." What could I do from my office? I had heard about violence in the workplace, but what about violence at home while you are at the workplace? Thank goodness I was able to talk Rachel out of knocking out her sister.

Rachel always hated doing dishes because of the "floaters," as she called them. Since this was one of her chores, I would frequently hear about it. I would tell her that if she would scrape the dishes first, she wouldn't have that problem. Apparently, her dislike for washing dishes was well known, because for her birthday one year, her friend got her a whole stack of paper plates. Problem solved—at least for the summer.

One morning Rachel was making herself an egg for breakfast. She had the egg in her hand, ready to put it in the skillet. Just then she sneezed. Her hand flew up, and the egg cracked on the range hood. There was salmonella running everywhere. That was an *egg*-specially bad day.

Another time Rachel dropped a can of cooking spray on the kitchen floor. We watched helplessly as the thing went spinning in circles out of control while spraying all over the place. It just about turned my kitchen floor into an ice skating rink. Believe the warning on the label—the contents of those cans are definitely under pressure.

Rachel was about thirteen when she called me at work and said, "Mom, I was going to make a cake, but we are out of eggs. Can I use cheese instead?" Even if she was making a cheesecake, I don't think that would work.

One of the things I learned from being a mother is never to allow a teenager to be interrupted by a phone call when cooking or a key ingredient may be left out. Let me just say we had Helper instead Tuna Helper that night. If you think it tastes bad with the tuna, you should try it without it.

Rachel has always liked food. Whenever she had to write something about herself in school, it would always start out something like this: *My name is Rachel. I like to eat.* Or, *I love stroganoff. I eat a lot.* She wrote a book about herself in school, and there were two whole paragraphs dedicated to cake. Part of it reads: *A lot of my friends like cake. I do, too! When my mom makes a cake, I eat five pieces of it. I ask my mom for chocolate cake mix and icing. Sometimes my mom says I eat too much, but I like eating!* One Mother's Day, Rachel wrote a letter to me that said, "I love you. You are better than chocolate." If that wasn't convincing enough, it was accompanied by a picture, and above it she wrote, "To a person better than chocolate."

Her love of chocolate is still strong today. When she got married, she was considering Hershey, Pennsylvania, as a honeymoon spot.

One time we were getting out of the car to grab some lunch when Rachel made the comment that she forgot the pot that was in her school locker. Her siblings and I realized she meant the clay pot she made in art class, but I'm not sure what the man who happened to be walking past us thought.

When Rachel had her wisdom teeth pulled, I stopped at the pharmacy on our way home to get her prescription. Rachel was still kind of groggy from being knocked out, so after several attempts to wake her with no success, I locked the car and went in to get her medicine. While I was gone, she apparently woke up and did not know where she was. When I got back to the car, she said I had abandoned her in her time of need. Not true, of course. She tried to talk to me on our drive home, but I could not understand her. I asked her to take the gauze out of her mouth and say it again. When she did, it was as bad without the gauze as it was with it.

***

When Rachel was about fourteen, she decorated her room with strings of white lights. She had placed them along the edge of her ceiling. One night she was asleep in her room, and I had fallen asleep on the couch. All of a sudden I was awakened by Rachel screaming that there were snakes hanging on her wall. As much as I hate snakes, in my sleepy state I headed toward her room to see what the problem was. I was in my stocking feet, and as I made way up the three steps to her room, I felt what I thought was a snake under my foot. I started screaming, she started screaming, and before long we had the whole household awake. At that point, I figured out that the snake on the stairs was actually a rolled-up sock. So I got my heart rate down and continued on to Rachel's room.

I asked "So where is the snake? Is it under your bed or in the closet?"

She said, "No, it's hanging on the ceiling."

On the ceiling, I thought. *What was it hanging on with—its little snake hands?* That was when reality set in. What Rachel had thought was a snake was actually a string of lights. Bad dreams can sure mess with reality.

***

My husband Eddie and I took the kids to Sea World In Sandusky, Ohio in 1999. We also had taken Nicki, who was a friend of my daughters', and the three of them were sitting in the stands a few rows down from me and Eddie. While waiting for the show to start, they were playing with a stretchy hair tie. Rachel had it between her two fingers, and Nicki was trying to pull it off. All of a sudden, the hair tie flew off Rachel's fingers, went behind the girls, bounced off a man's knee, and went straight down the back of the pants of a girl who was sitting in front of them. The girl never knew what happened. We thought it best not to ask for the hair tie back.

Rachel was a new driver and I was a passenger in the car when I saw a deer near the road. I didn't want to startle her while she was driving, but I wanted to make sure she saw it. So I said in a low voice, "Deer." No response. I repeated "deer" a few more times, and each time I raised my voice a little more. Still no response. Finally I yelled, *"Deer!"* That got her attention. I guess she thought I was saying "dear" all this time.

Rachel came home from work one day and said her car was making a weird noise. When I asked her what kind of noise, she said it sounded like metal hitting something, but she only heard it when she was moving. Her dad wasn't home yet, and I don't know anything about cars, but I told her to show me anyway. So we went outside, she started up her car, and sure enough, it was fine until she moved forward. It was then I realized what the metal noise was: her tire was not only flat but hanging off the rim. The metal sound we were hearing was the rim making contact with the road.

Rachel's first car was a used Dodge Neon. It had issues, including a strange odor we could never identify. Rachel got to the point where she hated the car. Finally she decided to sell it and get a better vehicle. We advertised it, and a young man came to check it out. After looking at it and taking it for a test drive, he asked, "Hey, did you know the brakes are bad?" We answered yes, we did. "Did you know the trunk leaks"'" We answered yes, we did. "Did you know it has a weird smell?" We answered yes, we did. The next thing he said was, "I'll take it." Sold!

I always wanted to meet my children's dates and know some vital information about them, including what kind of car they drove, just in case there was a problem. One time Rachel introduced me to her latest guy, and he said, "I don't have a car, but you can come check out my bike if you want to." I guess the word was out.

Rachel has always liked to talk—a lot. She's a nurse now, but I told her if that didn't work out, she could always become a telemarketer. I would buy something just to get her off the phone.

***

After dating her boyfriend for seven years, Rachel got engaged. For her bridal shower in 2013, I wanted to make her a cake. In the process, I was faced with several hurdles. First, I discovered I had no cake mix, so I had to run up to the store before I could even get started. I wanted the cake to be special, so to decorate it, I ordered a frosting sheet made from a picture that Rachel had e-mailed me of her and Jason, her husband-to-be.

I had used a frosting sheet previously on a cake I made for a friend of mine and had no problem at all. But that was not the case this time. I had trouble getting the film backing off of it once I was ready to place it on the cake. I followed all the directions that came with it, but I was having no luck. So I e-mailed the lady who made it for me and waited for a response. Finally, after getting no immediate answer, I tried getting the film off by placing a knife between the picture and the backing. Success! I positioned the picture on the cake just right. The lady finally e-mailed me back and said she forgot to mention the knife method.

I finished decorating the cake and lightly covered it with a piece of plastic wrap, being careful not to let anything touch the picture. Since I used my big cake pan, I had no other way to protect it. I put the cake in a safe place and thought that would be the end of worrying. When I looked at the cake a little later, I noticed the plastic wrap was touching the picture, so I attempted to gently lift it. Bad idea! When I did that, my future-son-in-law's face began coming up with the plastic. The more I pulled, the more his face disappeared. I was panicked. I tried to patch his face with some leftover frosting, but that only made an already bad situation worse. He ended up looking like a one-eared, one-eyed pirate.

Then I got what I thought was a good idea. I printed off the picture Rachel had sent me to use for the frosting sheet. I cut out Jason's head and used it to cover up the distorted one on the cake. It was obvious this was not a good match. The frosting sheet picture was a little bigger than the one I printed, so Jason's new head didn't quite fit on his old shoulders. But I was out of time for making a new cake, so I consulted my other daughter and decided I would just have to make the best of it.

I took it to the wedding shower and let Rachel know what had happened. Some of the guests had taken a glance at the cake but were too polite to tell me they noticed something weird. After a while, everyone knew the whole story about the cake. Jason's mom told me she thought that I had used Jason's face to cover up someone else whom Rachel had dated. We all ended up getting a good laugh out of the whole situation, including Rachel.

That same day, I had my blouse on inside out and didn't know it. Thank goodness neither did anyone else. In fact, I got compliments on it from several of the ladies at the shower, so I assume they weren't aware of my wardrobe malfunction. The blouse is called a popcorn blouse. It's kind of hard to explain, but it has puffy things all over it. The inside looks a lot like the outside. The only reason I knew I had it on inside out was because after I got home, I noticed that the seams on the shoulders were on the outside. That wasn't a good sign.

Rachel and Jason's wedding was beautiful, although there was that candle I couldn't get lit. At the wedding reception, all the single ladies were asked to come forward for the bouquet toss. My grandson, Adam, asked his dad if he was a single lady.

Since getting to know my son-in-law, I learned that when he was little, he went to his dad one day and said he needed a spanking. His dad asked him why. Did he do something bad? Jason said no, but he was getting ready to.

English-Challenged Mandy

The logic of children is always amusing, but Mandy's was especially entertaining. For example, she woke up crying one morning when she was a small child, and I asked her what was wrong. She said she had a bad dream. Wanting to reassure her and comfort her, I asked her what it was about. "Mom," she said with her little hand on her hip. "You know what it was about. You were in it!"

I went to Mandy's preschool Christmas program, where the children all sang "Rudolph the Red-Nosed Reindeer." When they got to the end where it says, "He'll go down in history," the lone voice of four-year-old Mandy sang out, "Like Michael Jackson!" I don't know where that came from.

We were eating dinner one evening when Mandy suddenly said she had a pea stuck up her nose. Sure enough, she did. It took some blowing, but it finally came out. After it was all over, I asked her how she managed to do that. Her answer was that she dropped it. Either that pea had quite a bounce, or the law of gravity wasn't present in our house. (I knew that house had issues!)

When Mandy was about four, I bought a Christmas stocking kit that I had every intention of making for her. However, once I got started, I discovered it was much more detailed than I had realized. Since I had young children and worked full time, it was hard for me to find the time to do the extensive embroidery that was involved. Several Christmases went by, and I still didn't have the stocking done. Finally, when she was about seven, Mandy came to me one day and said, "Mom, you don't have to worry about finishing my stocking. I made my own." With that she produced a one-sided stocking she had made out of construction paper. What a guilt trip. Mandy had long since grown up when I was cleaning out a closet. I found that stocking—still undone. I managed to finish it and gave it to Mandy for Christmas when she was twenty-one. Better late than never, I guess.

No matter how old the kids were, Eddie would always make the same comment when they would tell us what they wanted for Christmas: "Well, we'll have to check with Santa." Mandy was about ten when she came to me and said, "Mom, I don't believe in Santa any more, but don't tell Dad, because I think he still does."

Mandy has always loved horses. In fact, when she was little she would tell us she wanted to be one when she grew up. I think she may have traumatized our dog, because she liked to dress her up like a horse. Now I know why there is a need for an animal psychologist.

It was the morning of the first day of school when Mandy came out of her room screaming. I asked her what scared her, and she said it was her alarm clock.

Mandy woke up one morning and asked, "When will Dad be home with the pizza?" I told her he did get home—last night.

***

Mandy loved writing notes to the tooth fairy. Money was always the theme for these messages. They were usually written on envelopes so the funds could conveniently be put inside. Here is what one of those notes said:

"I don't care if you give me two dollars or three dollars but I really want 100 dollars but I know that you don't have that muck [much] money. I love tooth fairys be cus they have weegs [wings]. I really wanted to fly. I wish you have a happy Valentines."

Another one said: "Dear fairy I hope you give me a lot av money. I love fairys. I hope win your done ples sign your name rat [right] here."

Once she did something different and made a card out of paper. It read: "Since you do all the work I gave you a picture. It's a present. I hope you like it. Can you give me 2 dollars."

Lack of communication between a mom and dad can be costly: one time Mandy got double tooth fairy money.

***

Mandy has never totally understood the English language, even though she was born in this country and has lived here her whole life. It started from the time when she was very young. When she was about seven years old, she said, "Mom, I'm at the bottom of the dump."

My first thought was, *Oh my goodness, is she depressed? Does she need a doctor?* So I asked her, "What do you mean, you are at the bottom of the dump?"

And she said, "You know, Mom, how you eat and eat, and you never get filled up"

Oh, I was quite relieved when I realized she meant "bottomless pit."

***

One day Mandy said, "Mom, Hazel's outside."

I said, "Hazel? I don't know any Hazels."

She said "You know, Mom. It's when it's not raining, but it's not snowing, it's hazel."

***

At Christmastime, we always put garlic on our tree, according to Mandy, not garland.

One time she asked me if you have an invisible fence, do you also need an invisible dog?

Mandy came to me one day and said her shoulder hurt. The problem was, she was rubbing her elbow. If that's where her shoulder was, no wonder it was hurting.

We used to have a store in this area called Lazarus. When Mandy was little, she would call it Lizards R Us. I thought, *What would they sell—clothes for your pet lizard?* That's just creepy.

Mandy always did like to clean. (She doesn't get that from me.) When she would want to clean mirrors or glass, she would always ask me where the Window-X was.

One time I went to a nearby Amish community with Mandy and Rachel. On the way home, Rachel made the comment that she liked the Amish because they were down to earth. Mandy then asked, "What does that mean, Mom? Are they all short?"

Since Mandy obviously takes things so literally, I wonder how she felt years ago when her first grade teacher told the class that she would know if the students misbehaved, even if she had her back turned, because she had eyes in the back of her head.

***

Things didn't improve when Mandy got older either. When September 11 happened, she was twelve. A few days after that event, I told the kids were going to go shopping at Target.

Mandy got very upset and said "Mom, we can't go to Target, we just can't."

I said, "Why, what do you mean?"

She replied, "I heard on the news that the terrorists are going to bomb targets all across the United States!"

***

Mandy was a teen when I noticed her kind of chuckling while flipping through a magazine one day. I asked her what was so funny. She said, "I can't believe someone has a name like that."

I asked, "What is it?"

"Fobe."

I asked to see the magazine and started to laugh. It wasn't Fobe, but Phoebe. She said she didn't see the last e, but I don't think that would have made a difference.

***

Mandy was in high school when she and I went shopping at the mall. She saw a pair of shoes on the display rack that she thought were adorable, so she went to check them out. She came back disappointed and said, "Darn, I like these shoes, but they don't have my size." I had to inform her that it was just the display. I was sure they had more sizes available, probably even hers!

To this day, instead of saying it's not her cup of tea, Mandy says it's not her piece of cake. And instead of saying go-cart, she calls it goat-cart.

***

When Mandy went to get her oil changed and her tires rotated for the first time by herself, I asked her how it went when she got home. She said, "I am so mad, Mom."

I said, "Why, what happened?"

"I told them to rotate my tires, and all they did was take them off and move them around. I didn't see them spin them at all!"

I explained to her that moving the tires around *is* a tire rotation. Then Mandy said she knew what her problem was—it's because she is so liberal.

***

After graduating from college, Mandy got a job at a veterinarian's office and mistakenly read a cat's name as Stripper instead of Striper.

I wondered why Mandy always beat me playing cards when we are sitting on the couch. Then she confessed to me one day that she could see my cards in the reflection of my glasses, but she never looks. Yeah, right!

CHAPTER 3

CATS, DOGS, AND OTHER CRITTERS

Most children have had some kind of pet growing up. Mine were no exception.

When my son was young, we had a half-moon conure, a kind of parrot. My husband thought it was a little too noisy, so I took it to our neighborhood pet shop to trade it in on a quieter model. I came home with a cockatiel, which was supposed to be friendly and a little quieter than the parrot. Not ours! That was the meanest bird on two legs. He would even hiss when I tried to feed him. After we had him for a few days, we named him Killer. When we opened the cage door, he would sit there until our cat came in the room. Then he would swoop down low, but just high enough so the cat couldn't get him. I think the pet shop had him a little too close to the snake cages, because he had picked up a few bad habits.

One year when my son was little, he brought home some salamanders from school to take care of during his summer break. I wasn't crazy about the idea, but Robert did a good job watching after them. One time he brought them outside in a shoebox, and he dropped it. The salamanders started crawling off in all directions. The more Robert tried to avoid stepping on them, the worse it got. Unfortunately, the salamander population was a little lower after that day.

Robert also had a rabbit that started out teeny but ended up turning into Big Bubba. We kept him in a cage in our basement, and somehow he turned into quite an escape artist. One day the router to my TV antenna was not working, and I traced the cord down to the floor. It appeared to be cut—or bitten—in half. Then we found our rabbit. Apparently, he had gotten out of his cage, hopped up our basement steps, and started chewing.

One day Eddie came home from work and surprised us with a little puppy. We already had a dog, a cat, and my son's fish and gerbils. We named the new addition Scooter because he liked to scoot across the floor. Like all puppies, he liked to chew things, but the only clothes he ever chewed up were mine. He also liked to gnaw on me whenever my husband left the room.

Scooter soon grew into a huge dog, and Eddie built him a dog house for our tiny yard. One day I was at the grocery store buying pet food for our various pets. The lady behind me in the checkout line noticed and commented that I must be quite an animal lover. I got into a conversation with her, and it came up that Scooter was outgrowing our small house and yard. The lady expressed interest in adopting Scooter, and I jumped at the idea. A few days later, my new friend and her husband came over to our house, and they fell in love with Scooter. That's how he found a new home. I've never met anyone else who has managed to find their pet a new home while standing in a grocery line.

When my children were small, I had a dog named Peaches. She was a little odd looking, part Chihuahua and part poodle. She had a long tail and curly hair. I had a little girl ask me one time if she was a dog or a cat. I didn't think Peaches was ugly, but apparently I was alone in that thought. I wanted to get her trimmed up for summer one year, and the dog groomer refused to take my money. His message to me was, "If you think this dog is ugly now, just take off that fur. That's the only thing that gives her character." So that ended the new look for Peaches.

At the same time I had Peaches, I became the owner of a very nice stray cat that I named Muffin. The name seemed to fit, since it sounded girly and the cat had a very feminine meow. Then I got a phone call from the vet after I dropped Muffin off to be spayed. He said there was something he had to tell me. I was scared to think about what he was about to say. I thought the cat had died in surgery or something. Then the vet made the problem clear with one sentence: "We don't spay males." So from that day on, Muffin became Mr. Muffin.

One time I had to save the cat from Rachel's attempt at brushing his teeth. Mr. Muffin wasn't interested in that. The cat developed an allergy problem (maybe from toothpaste?), which resulted in a receding furline on his head and tail. I always hoped these two would never meet. He also had a fat lip periodically because of the allergies. Even my pets have issues!

***

One day I was picking up Peaches from a vet visit, and I gave my name to the lady at the desk. "Oh, are you here to pick up Muffin?" she asked.

"No," I replied. "That's my cat. I am here to pick up my dog, Peaches."

The next thing I know, a lady whom I have never met before in my life was standing behind me. "Peaches and Muffin," she said. "Do you always name your pets after food?" Then she said "My name is Smith. I am here to pick up my tiger cat. His name is Stripes."

I thought, *Really? A tiger cat named Stripes, and she has a problem with my pets' names? At least I am creative and I didn't name my all-gray cat Solid.*

***

After Mr. Muffin sadly died, I went to the local animal shelter to adopt another cat. I decided on an adult cat and came home with Babs. It should have been a sign of things to come when she nearly broke out of the cat carrier even before I got her home by banging her head into its door. I am sure Babs had a bad headache as a result.

She turned out not to be the nicest cat in the world. I found out pretty quickly that she did not like other animals or children. She liked to sit on the back of the couch and hiss at anyone who got near her. I think her previous owner must have been an old lady who hated kids. She even bit

51

me when I touched a sensitive spot on her back while she was lying on my lap. My husband had to actually pull her loose from the grip she had on my thumb. I had to go to the emergency room for treatment. After a while, she mellowed out somewhat and tolerated us just a little. She lived to be fifteen years old.

***

When Peaches was getting older, she had several health issues. I knew that she was in the yard as I was pulling my car into the garage. Suddenly I felt a bump, so I got out of the car to investigate. Peaches was lying behind my rear tire. I ran into the house and immediately called the emergency vet's office. The conversation went something like this:

Me: I would like to bring my dog in to be checked.

Vet: What seems to be the problem?

Me: I think I may have ran over her with my car.

Vet: What do you mean, you *think* you ran over your dog?

Me: I was pulling into my garage and felt a bump. When I looked back, my dog was lying behind my back tire. She's not flat or anything, but now she's having trouble walking.

There was a short pause before I heard the vet say, "Lady, if you even *think* you may have run over your dog, you need to bring her in."

As it turned out, she had coincidentally had a seizure behind my car. That was a relief knowing it was not my fault.

***

I had never met a hamster that hissed until Mandy had one. When she picked it out at the pet store, she couldn't wait to put it in its new home. But when she opened the box she'd carried it home in, the hamster started hissing. It broke Mandy's heart and about scared her to death. Maybe it thought it was a reptile instead of a rodent. Cinnamon was a very temperamental hamster.

***

When Mandy was about seven, she had another hamster she named Dusty. Dusty had an eye problem. At times his right eye would look like it was loose from the socket. We had to be careful when we cleaned the cage because it looked a lot like the droppings. One day Mandy came running out of her room saying Dusty had died. I tapped and shook the cage, and he didn't move. I also came to the conclusion that he was dead. (I wasn't about to pick up a dead rodent.) We found a little box to bury him in, and then I carried the whole cage down to the garage so Mandy wouldn't have to look at it until we could bury him the next day.

The next morning, I heard Eddie coming up the basement steps when he should have been leaving for work. To my surprise, he was carrying the hamster cage. I asked him why he was bringing that dead hamster back upstairs, and he showed me why—Dusty wasn't dead at all. I guess even hamsters can play possum. The poor thing had been in the thirty-degree garage all night. I thought for sure he would catch pneumonia and die anyway, but the hamster lived for several more years.

Rachel also had a hamster the same time Mandy did. One morning we found both hamsters missing, even though they were in different cages in different rooms. Apparently, they coordinated their cage breaks!

***

When my son was a teenager, he had a critter called a sugar glider. To me, it looked like a cross between a squirrel and a mouse. One time Robert had him under his shirt. My daughter came and slapped Robert on the back, not knowing what was hidden. We heard a squeal, but thank goodness no sugar gliders were hurt in this incident.

We had some other unusual pets too. Mandy always loved horses, so when she was in the sixth grade, we got her a miniature horse that she named Buddy. After that, we got two pygmy goats that we named Big Bob and

Little Bill to keep Buddy company. Sometimes, though, I think Buddy wished he was alone. Those goats could be annoying, like the time when they chewed off most of Buddy's tail. It happened right after Mandy groomed him, so I don't know if the goats were jealous of how good the horse looked or were just bored. In any case, Buddy ended up with about an eight-inch tail, not even long enough to shoo the flies away. It took awhile for his tail to fully grow back.

Goats are crazy little critters. We were gone for a while one day, and when we came back, one of the goats had a bucket stuck on his head. We don't know if it had been that way for five minutes or all day. Either way, the goat had no idea how to get it off.

I was out by the barn one day, just minding my own business, when something hit the back of my legs. The next thing I knew, I hit the ground. As I went down, all I saw was a white blur. I'm not sure if it was Big Bob, Little Bill, or my son's dog, but I blamed it on the goats. It was just something they would do.

***

Christine Hogalara and Sally Mae were our potbellied pigs. Sally Mae was the first one we got. She was needing a home badly. When I mentioned her situation to Eddie, he readily agreed to adopt her. When we first got her, Eddie had her living on our front porch "temporarily." She got very possessive of her living space and would chase us whenever they went out there. Eddie even built a ramp for her so she could venture out in the yard when she wanted to. I finally convinced him that Sally Mae would be perfectly happy in our barn, where he then made her a very nice living area.

I started getting a little worried with his obsession with Sally Mae. In the morning, he would share his coffee with her and feed her flavored marshmallows. He said she didn't like sink water, so he bought bottled water for her. He was going hog wild.

We got Christine a little later, after she outgrew a petting zoo. Eddie was kind of a pig whisperer. Christine and Sally Mae would follow him all over the yard, and he could get them to go back in the barn when no one else could.

One thing we learned about potbellied pigs is that periodically they need their hooves trimmed. We also learned that they can be stressed out very easily, which could cause death. When it came time to get their hooves done, the farrier suggested giving them a warm beer to relax them for the procedure. After several failed attempts to get them to drink the beer, we finally gave up. Buddy, however, wanted it in the worst way. He was on his knees trying to get into the pigs' stall so he could enjoy the beer.

Once my children got older and started losing interest in them, I decided to try to find Christine and Sally Mae a new home. I knew I would have to find just the right person to take them, since it wasn't like giving away a puppy or a kitten. Coincidentally, it was almost time for the county fair, so I decided to post a "free to a good home" notice and hope for the best. Surprisingly, someone actually responded and was interested in adopting them. A very nice couple came in a van, and we began the process of getting Christine and Sally Mae to go in. Easier said than done! The potbellies squealed and carried on like they were being led to the slaughter. It took awhile, but we finally got them in the van. The new owners said they would also take the goats if I was willing to give them up. So I accepted their offer. In contrast to the potbellies, we had no trouble getting the goats into the van. They must have sensed a road trip, and they were all for it, not even caring where they were going. That left Buddy, who stayed with us until Mandy went to college.

***

In 1992, when my daughters were very young, I decided to adopt a dog from the local animal shelter. My husband was working nights at the time, and I thought a dog would help us feel a little safer. I called the no-kill shelter and told them exactly what I was looking for. I wanted a small to medium adult dog that was housebroken and good with children and would also get along with my cat. The lady I spoke with said that a dog named Floppy would be perfect for us. So I stopped by the shelter and met the dog without the kids in case it didn't work out. I liked Floppy, and Floppy seemed to like me. I told the lady that I would be back in a few hours after I picked up my children from school. In the meantime, I stopped at the pet store to pick up a few items. When the time came, I picked up the kids and headed back to the animal shelter. Of course, my kids were excited about getting a dog.

Well, we were met with a whole new attitude when we returned. A lady with owl eyes that seemed to work independently approached our car, and we were not given the option of getting out.

She blocked my car door and said, "We've been thinking about it, and we don't think you are right for Floppy."

I was dumbfounded. I asked, "What do you mean? I was right for Floppy just a few hours ago."

"We don't think you're compatible," she said.

Not compatible? I thought. *I'm not looking for a date or a husband—I'm looking for a pet for my family.* "What about another dog?" I asked. "Can we look at some others?"

"No, we don't think you're compatible with any of our dogs."

Really—none of the forty in the shelter? I didn't know why she said that. After all, I've had pets my whole life. But there was no reasoning with the owl-eyed woman. I had to wonder, if the staff was that good at judging compatibility, why didn't they run a dating service for people? I never did understand it, but we left without a dog. I guess they were not just the no-kill shelter; they were also the no-adoption shelter. Ironically, we ended up adopting a dog, Leo, who was on the waiting list for that same place. It must be a long wait time if they don't allow adoptions.

Leo was a strange-looking dog (though not quite as strange looking as Peaches.) He was part basset hound and part whatever jumped over the fence. He had a long tail and stubby legs—and some strange habits. He would sneak into the bathroom, and we would see his tongue come under the shower door to drink the water while we took a shower. He also loved to eat whatever we were eating. He could sit and beg for minutes on end until he made us feel guilty enough to share our food with him. Then my husband would have to hold him up so Leo could see there was no more food on the kitchen counter. If we were eating grapes and one of them happened to fall on the floor, Leo would roll on it first, then eat it. One time I had just made a cake, put it on the table, and left the room for less than a minute. Just that quick, Leo managed to eat off a corner of it by jumping on the kitchen chair and helping himself to the cake.

He was also a chewer. He was a year old when we got him, and he was still chewing up stuff like toys, a Nintendo remote, crayons, and clothes. I don't know how his gastrointestinal system handled all that plastic.

Leo also liked to lie on his belly and let the kids pull him around the floor using one of his toys that he would hold in his mouth. Leo also liked to hide his treats. More than once I found a Milk-Bone or rawhide toy under my pillow. When I would be reading to the kids on the couch, he would come and squeeze in between us. If we told Leo it was time for bed, he would look at my husband as if asking permission to stay up longer. When my daughter, Rachel, was little, she used to say that Leo was like having another brother because he would get into trouble, make weird noises, and eat a lot.

As Leo got older, he had issues. He developed a weird body odor problem that even the veterinarian couldn't resolve. Also he needed some dental work done. He was knocked out for it, and when we brought him home, he staggered up the steps like a drunken sailor.

***

We got our dog, Snickers, in 1998 from our local IGA store. Someone was giving away puppies in the parking lot. Snickers is part border collie, and she is very sweet but very shy.

On this one particular day, Snickers was running around our coffee table, where Mandy happened to have her round curling brush. Snickers has a furry tail. I think she has my luck, because somehow the brush latched onto her tail and got stuck. Snickers was freaking out. The more she ran trying to get away from the brush, the more tangled it became. It took some time, but finally we got her to stop running long enough to get the brush out of her tail.

Snickers had an extra claw that caused her trouble, so we had the vet remove it. A few days later, she managed to pull the stitches out, and we had to take her to the emergency vet for treatment. This time she got one of those cones to keep her from biting that area again. When the vet put the headgear on her, I asked if Snickers was going to get laughed at when we went out to the waiting area, which was full of people. "Oh, no," the vet assured me. "We use these all the time." So we walked out, and the first thing we heard were some children *snicker*ing.

There was snow on the ground when we went left the vet's. As Snickers started sniffing the ground, she also started scooping up snow into her cone. And as with all dogs that get the dreaded cone, she could not judge her distance very well, so she had trouble maneuvering around the house. It was a bit entertaining.

One time I took Snickers to the vet to get her nails clipped. Before I could get her inside the office, she freaked out once she realized where she was. She wiggled out of her collar and ran right in the middle of the busy road, barely missed by oncoming traffic. Then she ran back to the side of the road and almost got hit again. From there she kept running and turned on a side street. I jumped into my car and followed her. I got some help from one of the drivers who had almost hit her, as well as the dog groomer from the vet's office. We saw Snickers run into the dense woods at the end of the side street, and then we lost sight of her. I called her name over and over again, but she would not come out. I couldn't believe my elderly dog was willing to run from me and possibly face spending her last years as a stray. The groomer assured me she would come out eventually, so I continued to call her. She stuck her head out once, but ran back into the woods. It was about forty-five minutes later when she finally came out and allowed me to pick her up. I guess she really didn't want those nails trimmed.

One day I let Snickers out to do her business. I got busy doing housework and forgot all about her. It started to storm when I finally remembered she was outside. In my rush to get the dog, I stepped on my cat's tail while going down the stairs. Poor Snickers looked like a drowned rat by the time I got her back in the house.

A few years ago, she had to have fourteen teeth removed. I don't know how many teeth dogs have, but I thought I was going to have to rename her Gumby.

Snickers is now sixteen years old, and Gordy refers to her as "Spot" because she basically lies in the same spot all day.

***

Sometimes we don't find our pets—our pets find us. In the spring of 1999, I had just picked my girls up from school for a doctor's appointment when a cat came out from under the shrubbery and began meowing at us. She looked pitiful. I wondered if she was a stray or if she belonged to someone. I had to decide what to do quickly, since we had an appointment to keep. I didn't want to leave her, but I also didn't want to take off with someone's pet. (I wouldn't want to be accused of being a cat burglar.) I decided to take my chances and bring her home. I put her in my van, dropped her off in our yard, and then took the kids to the doctor's. I decided if the cat was still there when we got home, so be it. Sure enough, she was. I checked with the school and was told she was a stray and had been there for some time, so we adopted her. We named her Lucy. She joined our furry family, which at that time included Leo and Snickers.

Our pet population has grown since then. Every time we bring home a new pet, Lucy just gives us that look like, *Oh no, not again!* She has always wanted to be the only pet. Good luck with that. She tolerates the others, but lets them know she needs her space. Gordy refers to Lucy as "Fossil" because of her age. She is about sixteen now, and she has gotten a little weird in her old age. She likes to sit on the roof of my house, and she also has developed a taste for ranch Doritos. If I am eating them, she will be in my face until I give her some.

***

In 2003, when she was seventeen, Rachel was working at the flea market. She came home one night and told me that someone was giving away puppies; she wondered if I would like one. I thought it was funny that we would get a dog from the *flea* market. I don't remember saying it, but I must have asked for the biggest, hairiest, stupidest dog in the litter, because that's what I got. (When my coworker heard me describe the dog, she thought I was talking about her husband.) Bear is part collie and part German shepherd. Everyone who knows about dogs has told me she must be very smart with that bloodline. Well, Bear must have missed that lesson. She is an idiot wrapped in a moron. We named her Bear since that's what she looks like. I think she's really part wolf. She has heavy collie fur, so in the summer when we trim her, she doesn't even look like the same dog. She looks more like a Doberman, which is good if she gets get out of the yard and starts terrorizing the neighborhood. I could always deny ownership and say that's not my dog.

A few weeks after we brought her home, I put Bear outside in a fenced area. It started to rain, so I went out to get her and discovered she had managed to get her head stuck in the fence—upside down. I thought we were going to have to use the little Jaws of Life (aka pliers) to get her out.

Besides not being too smart, she is also the nosiest dog I have ever met in my life. If she were a person, you wouldn't be able to stand her. One time I was looking for her in the house and could not find her. I knew she had to be somewhere. I called her but got no response. I finally found her in the bathroom. It seems she was being her usual nosy self and had stepped into the shower. The folding door closed behind her, and she could not figure out how to get out. So she just stayed there until I found her.

I have heard chocolate kills dogs, but I'm not sure if that's true. Bear has eaten so many stolen chocolate cookies, and she is still alive and kicking. She has stolen Oreos, Chips Ahoy, chocolate bars, etc. She even stole a cookie I had in my purse and managed to leave the wrapper in place. Every now and then I wonder (not seriously, of course) if that antifreeze rumor is true. Maybe I should give Bear some to wash down all that chocolate!

Bear likes to make us feel guilty when we eat in front of her. She will stare at us, and then occasionally we will feel drool on our leg. When Bear eats, it's always like it's her last meal. She just gobbles it down—I don't think she even chews it. I can tell because of how it looks when she hacks it back up. Like the day when Gordy came into the room and startled her.

Bear loves to check out the trash. She treats it like her own personal feeding bowl. One time I caught her with a discarded roll hanging out of her mouth, and she just froze. I guess she thought that if she didn't move, I wouldn't be able to see her. There was a time when I had done some baking and I threw the excess flour in the trash. Bear got into it, and when she got done, she looked like a cocaine-sniffing drug dog. Her nose and mouth were completely white.

During the Christmas season one year, we came home to what was left of my battery-operated tea lights. Bear must have been attracted to them because they were cinnamon scented and, of course, she cannot pass up food, even if it's fake. One Thanksgiving, I accused my husband of throwing the turkey carcass in the trash can because we woke up to bones everywhere. When Gordy assured me he was not at fault, we figured out that Bear somehow managed to stand on her hind legs and get it off the stove, even though we had pushed it all the way back.

I have thought about putting Bear in a box with a sign that reads "Free to a Good Home". If that gets no results, I could change it to "Free to a Home". One last revision would just read "Free".

Bear seems to be very self-centered. When she runs, she has no regard for anything or anyone in her way. She has run over Snickers more than once.

And Bear hates storms. The first sound of thunder, and she turns into a Jell-O mold. She shakes and shivers and wants to be a lap dog. She will not let us out of her sight. One day I was afraid I was going to have to take her to work with me because it was storming and she did not want me to leave the house. She followed me down to the garage, and we went around and around my car several times before I got her back in the house. One time while she was being boarded at a kennel for a few days, a bad storm came through the area. When I picked her up, the groomer, whose residence is above the facility, told me she was so nervous that he felt sorry for her and allowed her to stay in his home that night. Proof that even dogs can be scaredy-cats.

***

In the winter of 2007, we went through a deep freeze. In February of that year, we had a snow and ice storm that resulted in power outages in our neighborhood. My electric was out; therefore, I also had no water and no heat. (Even though I was a recent utility company retiree, my electric was out just the same.) At the time, I had three dogs—my ten-year-old dog Leo, my little dog Snickers, and big, hairy Bear. I felt sorry for them, especially Leo, because he was old and just about hairless. I thought he was going to turn into a Pupsicle, he was shivering so badly. I decided to take the three of them to my vet's and board them until my electric and heat came back on. (I was tempted to ask if they boarded people too. At least it would be warm there.) So I loaded up the dogs, put my car heater on full blast, and headed out.

Bear hogged all the heat on the way there. She sat on the front seat like a person with her butt on the seat and her front legs on the floor and put her nose on the vent where all the heat was coming from. So Leo continued to shiver all the way to the kennel. Once we got there, I took Snickers out first on the leash to take her inside. She got nervous and wiggled out of her leash and began running loose on the parking lot. I finally caught her and had her in my arms when I found the only patch of ice in the parking lot. I fell on my knee, but somehow I managed not to drop Snickers. The owner of the kennel came out to help me, and as he took Snickers from me, I guess she got nervous again because she doggie doo'd all over my jeans! I got it off as best I could, got the other two dogs into the kennel, and then realized I'd forgotten their dog food. Rather than go all the way back home to get it, I decided to stop at the dollar store and pick some up. Because of the condition my pants were in, I am sure they couldn't wait for me to get done shopping. I hope I never have to go back to that particular store again, and I am sure they feel the same way.

***

Shortly after I married Gordy, he remodeled my kitchen. Our house is not big. My kitchen is right off my living room. Any normal living thing, whether it is a person or a dog, would be able to figure out how to get from point A to point B. Well, not Bear. I don't know if it's the new floor or just the new look in general, but every time she comes into the kitchen from outside, she gets a confused look on her face, and then she slides all over the place trying to find her way to get into the living room.

One Christmas, Gordy's sister had a white elephant exchange at her house. Too bad it wasn't a brown dog exchange—maybe I could have wrapped up Bear.

In 2012, Gordy felt like he got an early Christmas present when Mandy decided to take Bear to live with her—after making sure that her apartment complex accepted big, hairy dogs. So we packed Bear's bags and said good-bye. Shortly after that, Mandy told me she was taking Bear for a walk, and there was a little gray-haired lady walking behind them. Bear went crazy with excitement. According to Mandy, Bear thought it was me. She almost dragged Mandy down trying to get to this person. She is just going to have to realize that there are more little old ladies out there besides me.

***

Around 2006, I acquired another pet when Rachel called from her apartment and said someone had just thrown a cat in a carrier in the dumpster outside. She couldn't keep him, so I told her to bring him to me. We named him DC, short for Dumpster Cat. He is quite the hunter, killing anything that moves in the yard. Now we call him Demon, even though he is very sweet and loving.

DC loves to sit in any kind of vehicle. I always have to warn people who come the house to make sure they are not taking home a cat. One day I went out to my car and found Bear in the driver's seat and DC in the passenger seat. Were they waiting on a road trip? Maybe Bear heard about that one-way trip I always threatened to take her on.

***

How does the runt of the litter turn out to be the biggest? In 2009, Mandy's friend's cat had kittens, and Mandy talked me into getting one. I had the white one picked out, but Mandy wanted the gray one, which happened to be the smallest kitten. When we held her, she seemed to fake narcolepsy. She would immediately fall asleep in our arms. That stole our hearts, so we decided on her. We named her Charlie.

From day one, Charlie never did clean herself very well. When she ate as a kitten, there would be food particles left on her face. Now it's even worse because she is so fat she can't reach a lot of places. I call her Tubbs because of her size. When she lays on her side, only two legs are on the ground. When she "runs," it looks more like a roll, because her legs become hidden. She looks like a ball with feet. I feel like I need a back brace when I pick her up. She's a little lazy too. A few times I caught her eating while lying on her side with her head in the food bowl.

***

Since I knew Gordy was not a fan of pets, I was naturally surprised when he told me about some kittens he saw when he spotted a Land Rover that was for sale in 2013. While talking to the owners about the vehicle, he found out that the kittens were needing homes. I was shocked when he told me I could have one. I was thinking either he did something bad I hadn't found out about yet, or he really did love me.

A few days later, he went back to look at the vehicle again, and I went with him to check out the kittens. I picked out two that I really liked, and I could not decide which one I wanted. Now for the most surprising part of this story: I came home with two kittens that day. As I told Gordy, "We can't just get one. It needs a friend." So I brought them home to join our other three cats and our dog. I was trying to think of names for our new furry additions. Gordy suggested that since he was looking at a Land Rover when he found them, that should be their names—Land and Rover. I don't think so. I ended up naming them Mindy and Tippy. Mandy said that having five cats officially made me a crazy cat lady.

***

Besides my own cats, there have been others who have tried to make my home their home. When we first moved here in 1988, there were many cats hanging around. When I would call mine, ten others would come running. One time a mother cat had kittens inside the wall of our garage. There was a hole that she managed to squeeze through, and I began to hear meowing coming from inside the wall. Being an animal lover, one day I stuck my hand in to see if I could pet the little ones. When I did that, I heard screeching and scratching. When I brought my hand out, I was counting my fingers. That was the last time I tried that.

A few years ago, we had a very nice black cat show up at our house. We named him George. The funny thing about him was he was friendly as could be when I would let him in the house. But when he was outside, he acted scared like he didn't know us. Weird.

With all the cats I have, it would seem I would never have a pest problem. That is not always the case. One morning I got up to use the bathroom, and there was a mouse in the toilet. I don't know how it made it past all the cats, but obviously they were sleeping on the job. I was just glad I looked before I sat. I didn't know what to do about the situation, so I grabbed my hot dog tongs and retrieved the mouse from the toilet. Then I ran downstairs, opened my back door, and threw it out into the yard. I watched as it started to run away. It was so cold that morning I worried that the mouse was going to freeze, since it was dripping wet. I then realized it had worse luck than me—one of my cats ran over and finished it off.

Whenever I am asked if I'm afraid of spiders, I always say no. That's because if I were, I would never be able to go in my basement. I have seen some strange-looking spiders down there. One time I was taking laundry out of the washer and a spider crawled out with it. It was amazing enough that it survived being in the water, but how did it survive the spin cycle?

I am terrified of snakes. One time I was almost to the steps leading to my basement when I spotted a snake slithering down them. I panicked. No one else was home at the time, so it was up to me to solve the problem. I ran upstairs and got my trusty hot dog tongs and a shoebox. I rushed downstairs and, to my horror, the snake was gone. I knew it was somewhere in my basement. After looking around for a few minutes, I did manage to find it. I grabbed it with the tongs, threw it in the box, and got it outside. And I only screamed once.

Another time I went in the basement and discovered a snake that was stuck on duct tape that was holding some wires in place for my husband's computer. It was trying to get free, but all it could do was wiggle around. Again, where were my hot dog tongs? Thankfully, my son was there. He took over for me. By the way, if anyone wonders what to get me for Christmas, I can always use hot dog tongs. After snake duty, I don't reuse them!

When my children were little, we had a kiddie pool out in the yard. By the end of summer, it was looking pretty bad, and it was overtaken by frogs. One day I came home after picking my daughters up from the babysitter's, and they immediately ran over to the pool to see how many frogs were there. To our surprise, there were none. Then Rachel picked up the side of the pool, and we realized why. There was a huge snake lying there. Rachel screamed, which caused the rest of us to do the same.

One day I was sitting on the porch talking on the phone and had the door that leads to the living room open. I noticed my cat, DC, out in the yard, and he appeared to have a snake that he was flipping around. I didn't worry, since he was outside and I was safe on my porch. I continued talking on the phone, and before I knew it, DC not only brought the snake on the porch but proceeded to bring it into my house and drop it on my living room floor. I was hoping the snake was dead, but no. It began to move once he set it down. I screamed into the phone and told the person to hold on while I dealt with the situation. I hurriedly scooped up the snake into my dust pan and ran outside with it, hoping to dump it in my neighbor's yard. Well, I dropped the snake before I made it that far. It was probably slithering once more in my own yard. I was just hoping it didn't have brothers and sisters and a big mama somewhere.

My most recent "critter" story involves an unidentified hanging object in one of the trees on my yard. Gordy and I were doing some yard work when he noticed it. He asked me what I thought it was, and I said it looked like a possum, although it was pretty decomposed. Upon getting a closer look, my guess was correct. Apparently, it got its foot stuck in a fork in a branch and was unable to get free. So it hung upside down by its tail and foot until it died. What's even more amazing is the fact it hung there all winter unnoticed, even though it was close to the driveway. Now we have a bony, rotten, half skeleton hanging in the tree. We couldn't wait for spring to come and the leaves to hide it. If you think possums are ugly when alive, you should see this one!

***

I just had to add this last story. Gordy began to notice that our kittens were spending more time away from home and suspected that our neighbor may be feeding them something better than the dry-food diet I had them on. He suggested that I buy some tastier wet food so it would be an incentive for them to spend more time at our house. What? This coming from my self-proclaimed anti-pet husband? Can it be his days as "Old Yeller" are coming to a close? Only time will tell.

CHAPTER 4

ODD JOBS

Clowning Around

I have had several fun but unusual part-time jobs. Thanks to my answering an ad in the paper, one of those jobs is being a clown. My career started out at the age of forty-six and continues on today. My first clown name was Drop-Zee. My supervisor at work suggested that name because he said I was always dropping things.

While working as Drop-Zee at a company outing one time, I heard a lady announcing me this way: "Bring your children over to see Dumpster the clown. She is here making balloon animals." I can't speak for anyone else, but I would not let my children go see anyone named Dumpster. That wasn't the first time people got my name wrong. At other events I had been called Dipsy and Droopy—both of which probably were true by the end of the day!

This next incident happened when I arrived at a residence for a little girl's birthday party. I knocked on the door, greeted everyone, and walked across a crowded room to set up. That's when one of the parents (a man) said, "Hey, the adult entertainment doesn't start until later." I just laughed and continued setting up, although I was wondering about that odd comment. Then one of the women asked if I needed help. I told her I did not and continued on. Suddenly, the big bow in the back of my costume felt like it wasn't lying down right, and I reached back to push it down. That's when horror struck! My big three-foot-long zipper had separated, and my dress was open in the back, exposing my skin and my bra. That explained the man's earlier comment. I was so embarrassed. I apologized over and over while the mom of the little girl tried to pin me up. I went on with my show—what else could I do?—even though the pin-up job didn't work 100 percent. Anyway, when I got done, I still managed to get a twenty-dollar tip. But I'm not sure if it was a pity tip from the women or a "thanks for the cheap thrill" tip from the men. Anyway, I felt like I may have entertained the kids and the adults (at least the men) at the same time.

Now my clown name is Klara-Bella. I still put on my makeup and my blue hair, and I drive from my home to wherever the event is located. I also wear my red shoes, which were purchased at Shoe Carnival. Where else would a clown shop for shoes? My children have always been embarrassed by this, especially when they were in school. They did not like their friends to see their mom out in public in this condition. I told them at least I'm not out robbing banks or something. My daughter, Rachel, said, "Mom, we'd rather you did!"

Whenever I am at an event in my clown gear, one of the most-asked questions by the children is what kind of car I drive. They always assume it's one of those tiny clown cars used in the circus when in fact, for a long time, it was a minivan.

When I become Klara-Bella, there is a lot of makeup involved. One time I finished a party, came home, and had to go to the grocery store. I cleaned off my makeup and checked with my kids to make sure it was all off. They assured me I was fine. I believed them. While doing my shopping, I happened to run into some people I know, and we talked for a bit. When I got into better light, I realized I still had makeup residue on my face— black around my eyes and a white pasty look. I looked like a green-eyed ghoul. I'm afraid to think what my friends thought.

I like to be punctual when I am Klara-Bella. No one likes the clown to be late. I once took that thought to a whole new level when I showed up at a church festival a week early. I was all dressed up with no place to go.

I mean, where could I go after that? It's not like I could go shopping and blend in.

When I am Klara-Bella, I have a set time-frame when I will be working. I have to know when to cut the line of waiting kids, which is generally long. Sometimes that can be difficult. I have thought about pulling off my wig when my time is up, which would work for sure, but I wouldn't want to be responsible for any mental damage it would do to the kids. There are already enough scary movies about clowns for that. One year I did balloon animals for the kids during an Easter egg hunt at our local park. I had a very long line. I told my friends if I wasn't at church the next day, I was probably still there doing balloons.

Gordy and I have incorporated Klara-Bella into his winemaking. For our label, we used a picture of him sitting next to me as Klara-Bella with words that read, "Funny-Tasting Wine Made by Funny-Looking People"

Easter Bunny Blues

My other fun but short-lived job was being the Easter bunny on the mall. I would put on the bunny suit and heavy head, which had tiny eye holes that were hard to see through. Then I would be led out to the mall area, where I was supposed to sit in a chair and wait for the kids to come and get their picture taken with me. About my second day doing this, it was not very busy. The photographer and assistant were chatting and not paying attention to what was happening to me when I caught a glimpse of several teenagers approaching me. I was in trouble. My colleagues had their backs turned to me as I tried to hold my head on with my big paw hands while the kids were trying to pull it off! It was quite a struggle. I tried to get the attention of the photographer or the assistant, but my yells were muffled and unheard because of the heavy head. That's the day I turned in my bunny ears and ended my career as the Easter bunny. It was a hare-owing experience.

CHAPTER 5

SHARON STORIES

These stories show how everyday experiences for anyone else can turn funny and bizarre for me.

Once my son, Robert, had outgrown his first bicycle, I decided to place an ad in the paper to sell it. The bike was made for either a girl or a boy. The ad was to read: 16" unisex Schwinn bicycle, $45. After the paper came out, I started getting all kinds of weird phone calls. I couldn't figure out why until I checked my ad. The way it was printed, it looked like unisex had nothing to do with the bike. In addition, it had not only my phone number, but my address and a bunch of random numbers and symbols. Of course, my ad was the only abnormal one.

***

When Robert was about five, I was involved in a showdown with a city bus. I had a truck at the time, and I had just picked my son up from the babysitter's. We were approaching an intersection when a bus coming the opposite direction started turning the corner. The streets in the area were narrow. There were parked cars on the bus's side of the street, so the cars in my lane began backing down the road to make room for the bus to get through.

When it was my turn, however, I would not do it. I just sat there. I had all the time in the world. Unlike the other driver, I did not have a busload of cranky people. Before long, there was traffic stopped in both directions and spectators began to gather on the sidewalk to see what would happen next. After a while I decided enough was enough. So I got out of my truck, walked up to the house we were stopped in front of, and asked the person who answered the door to call the police.

"Is there an accident?" I was asked.

"No," I said. "There is a bus out there that won't move." The person gave me a perplexed look, but made the call.

When the little white metro car showed up (aka bus police), my son thought for sure we were going to jail. The officer went up to the bus driver and asked, "So what's going on here?"

He said, "That's her truck, and she won't move it."

Then he asked me the same question, and I said, "That's his bus and he won't move it." The officer asked why I wouldn't move my truck, and I told him that I was being asked to do something that was against all the driving rules I was ever taught. Nowhere in the driving manual did I see where you had to back down a street so a bus could get through. After a few minutes, I guess I successfully pleaded my case, because the officer said he was going to instruct the bus driver to continue on his way. I told him to make sure the bus didn't hit my truck as he passed. It was a tight squeeze, but the bus made it.

About a week after this incident, my son was riding his bike on the sidewalk in front of our house. After a little while, he came inside and said, "Mom, I saw that bus driver."

I knew exactly who he was referring to. "You did?" I asked.

"Yes," he said. "He went like this." He waved his hand. "But I went like this." He shook his fist. Whether that story is true, I don't know. But either way, it was a reason for me not to like buses.

***

Once when Robert was little, he came home from a carnival with a goldfish that he had won. I was getting ready to go to my mom's for Mother's Day, so I hurriedly prepared some water for the little fish so we didn't leave him in the plastic bag. I boiled some water to purify it (was that necessary?) and let it cool so I could transfer the fish. I guess I didn't wait quite long enough. When I put the fish in the fishbowl, he suddenly turned upside down and didn't look so good. So I took the fish out of the hot water back into the cold water, which was not the best thing to do. I think it was in shock.

Somehow the fish did survive. To protect the fish from our cat, I took it into my son's room, closed the door behind me, and set the fishbowl on my son's dresser. Then Robert and I went to my mom's as planned. We got home late that night, and Robert was asleep. So I carried him into his room, closed the door so the cat wouldn't follow us, and put my son to bed.

This is where the problems began. When I went to open the door, the doorknob fell off—on my side of the door. I was stuck in my son's room with him and the fish. I didn't know what to do. The neighborhood was dark—like I said, it was late. The only thing I could think of was to open the window and start yelling, which is what I did. Which resulted in me waking my son. Thankfully, my next-door neighbor heard my call of distress and came to my rescue. Fortunately, my back door was unlocked, so my neighbor was able to get in the house. She and I put our doorknob halves together, and we opened the bedroom door. I was released. Free at last!

***

We were in the middle of a drought one year when my children were small. It was so hot I decided to take them swimming at Coney Island. It managed to rain that day, even though there was only a 20 percent chance.

Getting the right pumpkin for Halloween is a very important event for children. In 1997, I took my kids to the same pumpkin patch that we had visited for the past five or six years to pick out our special pumpkins. We rode out to the huge field on a wagon that was being pulled by a tractor. Once we got to the field, it took awhile for my children to pick the pumpkin of their choice. Then we all got back on the wagon for the return trip. For most people, this would have been an uneventful ride. But not for us. We hadn't gone very far when we felt a big bump. I thought we had just gone over a ridge or a big rock in the field, but as my luck would have it, one of the wheels fell completely off of the wagon. The surprising thing was, the driver didn't even notice. He kept on going, and we had to yell for him to stop. We were told by the driver that had never happened before. So we all exited until the problem could be solved. I was hoping we wouldn't have to walk all the way back because my children, of course, had chosen the biggest pumpkins they could find. It would be impossible to carry them back to our destination. Fortunately, the driver of the tractor radioed back to our starting point, and another wagon was sent to rescue us.

About a week after this, my son wanted to go to a Halloween event called "Terror in the Country." After meeting him at his apartment with my daughters, we drove about an hour to find that "Terror in the Country" was not happening that year.

***

Back in the '90s, I went to an outdoor Neil Diamond concert at Riverbend with my friend, Terri. I wore my stylish jelly shoes. We were sitting there for a few minutes when Terri asked, "Hey, Sharon, do you smell something burning?"

And I said, "Yeah, it kind of smells like rubber." At that point I looked down and saw the toe of my shoe smoldering. We could actually see a little stream of smoke. Apparently, we had sat near some smokers who weren't watching where they were putting their hot butts, and my shoe managed to make contact with one. I started stomping my foot, but that didn't help. In fact, the extra oxygen only helped fuel the fire. No one sitting around us seemed to notice or care. I guess they thought all that foot tapping was me getting into the music. Finally I managed to put my toe out. Thank goodness no soles were lost!

***

One morning I couldn't find my hairbrush but did see one on the coffee table. My girls were young at that time and since they were always borrowing mine, I thought I would just use that one until mine showed up.

I was just about to put it in my hair when my daughter, Mandy, said, "Mom, don't use that brush."

"Why not?" I asked.

"Because," she said, "that's the one I've been using on the dog." Mandy saved me that day, but I had used that brush the previous day. That explained the itching I experienced for the next week.

***

In 1990, when my daughters were two and four, I took them to a watch a parade. Candy was passed out to the kids, and Rachel gave me hers to keep for her. I still had my work clothes on, so I stuck it all in my skirt pocket. Later I washed the skirt. It was halfway dry in the clothes dryer before I began wondering whether I had removed the candy. I hadn't, so my skirt pocket was permanently sealed with gum. Fortunately, it didn't ruin anything else.

For Christmas one year I wanted to get my children an easel. The box it was in was huge, and when I put it on top of my shopping cart, it was hard to see in front of me. I had to be careful not to hit something or someone as I made my way cautiously to the checkout. Once out of the store, I don't know why, but I had trouble finding my vehicle. Everyone else knew it too, because I found myself walking toward the store with the easel still on top of my cart. Finally, I located it. I got my keys out of my purse and opened up the back of my van. Then I put the keys back in my purse. The weather was bad, and there were icy spots in the store parking lot, so I had to try and keep the cart from slipping away on the ice. After struggling a bit, I managed to get the easel in my van, only to realize my purse was in the there as well, and it was under the easel! That meant my keys were under it too. I had to try and keep my balance on the ice while I worked to get my purse back out.

***

In the summer of 1996, I helped chaperone a camping trip for my daughter's Girl Scout troop. We were at the local state park. Skunks started raiding our area every night and got into any food that was left out.

The second night, Mandy and I slept in my car because it had rained the night before and our sleeping areas were wet. Without the use of a flashlight, the park was pitch black at night. Everything was fine until I felt something wet on my cheek. So I did what anyone would do—I started screaming. In my mind, one of those critters managed to get in my car. I scared Mandy, so she started screaming too. As it turned out, the wet feeling was just Mandy bending over to kiss me on the cheek before she went to sleep. I felt bad mistaking my child for a woodland creature, but how was I to know it wasn't a skunk?

We also had one girl in our group who was absolutely petrified of tree frogs, and they were everywhere in the restrooms. Also, my daughter, Rachel, hurt her toe and got burned with grease while cooking. Mandy got a nosebleed and said her horse bit her after she finished horseback riding. Other than that, everything went fine.

***

In 2000, I went with my family to Cincinnati's annual Labor Day fireworks display down at the riverfront. This event attracts thousands and thousands of people, and I had never had a problem in the many times I attended. This particular time was different, however. After the fireworks were over, the crowd was dispersing, and we were walking back to our car. All of a sudden I got the sensation that a cloud was passing over me. I looked up to see a giant shoe coming over the crowd and careening toward me. *Why would anyone throw their shoe into a crowd this size,* I wondered. The shoe looked like it was at least a size thirteen. Before I could do anything— *thump*--it hit me on the head and just about knocked me out. After I regained my senses, I realized how bad my luck really was that out of all those people, I was the one who was struck.

***

I had to go to my bank one day and make a car payment. I decided to use the drive-through. So I drove up with intentions of putting the paperwork in the tube and sending it on its way to the bank. When I reached out to get the tube, it slipped from my hands and dropped to the ground. It sounded like it rolled under my car. I wondered what I should do next. I decided to roll forward very slowly and listen for any crunching sounds that might be the tube being crushed under my tire. I proceeded forward and, thank goodness, I didn't hear any breakage. I parked my car, got out, and looked around for the tube. I found it in the parking area and started walking it back to the drive-through.

Meanwhile, a lady had pulled up into my spot, and she was getting ready to do her banking. I can't describe the look on her face when she saw me walking toward her holding the tube. I explained the situation and asked this person whom I had never met before if my payment could share her transaction. She looked at me like I might be crazy, but then agreed. I was able to get on with my life.

***

Years ago I went to the ATM on a Sunday to get some cash. As soon as I inserted my card, I heard a terrible noise. I knew it wasn't a good sign. Sure enough, the cover rolled down, and the ATM was done as far as I was concerned. It not only kept my card, it destroyed it. I had to wait for a week to get a new one in the mail. I couldn't understand why it did that to me when another customer used it right before me and the cover rolled back up for the person to use it after me. But then I remembered my luck.

When my daughter, Mandy, was in high school, I would occasionally drop her off on my way to work so she wouldn't have to ride the school bus. After she got her driver's license in 2004, I would sometimes allow her to do the driving. One particular morning, I grabbed my sweater, and after Mandy drove to school, I took over the wheel and drove to work. It wasn't until I got to work that I realized the arm of my sweater had been hanging out of my car all the way there. Apparently, I had closed the door on it when I switched from the passenger seat to the driver's side of the vehicle. To make it worse, it had been raining, so that part of my sweater was all wet and drippy most of the morning. Soggy is not a good feeling.

***

Right before Easter in 2006, I was leaving my house to go to work. I started down the steps to my garage and somehow I missed one. Before I knew it, I was at the bottom of the stairs. It felt like I had broken my foot. Luckily for me—and unluckily for her—my daughter, Mandy, was home because she had just started her spring break from school. She drove me to the emergency room, where the x-rays confirmed that I did indeed break my foot. To this day she still tells me that I did it on purpose just to mess up her school break.

I was wrapped and given crutches, which for me ended up being lethal weapons. They were just handed to me, like I knew what I was doing. I needed a five-foot radius around me just for the safety of others. I told the hospital attendants that if I was on them very long, they had better be prepared for more patients. As usual, the time spent in the emergency room was quite lengthy. Now I know why they keep asking you the same questions, like how old you are. By the time you get out, it *is* possible you may have had another birthday.

When we did finally get out of the ER, Mandy and I were both hungry and decided to get breakfast. Without thinking, we ended up at IHOP of all places. I managed okay on the crutches until I went into the restroom. I got in, but getting out was not so easy. I had to wait for someone else to need the facilities because I needed about two more hands to keep my balance, hold the crutches, and open the main door to the restroom. Thank goodness it was during their busy time, so I didn't have to wait long.

A few days later, when I went to get fitted for my walking shoe, my daughter took me to the orthopedic place. I hopped up to the handicap doors, pushed the button, and as the doors swung open, I was horrified to see them swinging right at me. I think I may have broken a land-speed record for hopping on one foot as I frantically tried to get out of the way before I got knocked down by a mechanical door. There must be a camera set up there so the people inside have entertainment watching people like me. I decided that there was a reason why those are called handicap doors. If you are not handicapped when you get there, you will be when you leave.

Somehow I survived the doors, the broken foot, and being driven around by a teenager for a few weeks. But I'm still not sure which of the three was worse. I thought this was the end of the saga. That was wishful thinking. Not only were my crutches from the emergency room adjusted wrong, but I had been fitted with the wrong size walking shoe at the orthopedic place.

My coworkers adjusted my crutches, and after developing a blister on my foot, I got a different size walking shoe. Those are the breaks!

Shortly after this, my son did some work on my porch and was going to replace some old, ugly '70s bushes, as he called them. Robert and I went to a landscaping place to get some ideas. One of the workers there told us to watch out for sinkholes. We began walking around, and when I came to a big puddle, I decided to go around it. I took one step onto the ground and my left foot, the one I had broken, immediately sank down into the mud about two feet. I was stuck and thought it was going to take the Jaws of Life to save me. Fortunately, Robert did manage to pull me out. Of course, my shoe fell off in the process. We both just laughed. What else could we do?

Out of Town Adventures

My luck is no better away from home. In the summer of 1990, my mom and I took my children to SeaWorld in Sandusky, Ohio. Back then there was no GPS, but we did have AAA. The route we were given by that agency did not exactly match the real world. We went too far north and ended up in Cleveland, which was about twenty miles too far. Then the two-bedroom suite we had reserved was being used by someone else when we arrived. So we were put in a smaller room, which we were told would be only temporary. As it turned out, it was permanent, because every time we asked about our room, we were told it wasn't ready. So we stayed in the smaller room and saved a little money.

My daughter, Rachel, was four during this trip and a bit accident prone. On the first day, while walking through the hotel lobby, she managed to knock over one of those tall, killer ashtrays with the sand that was situated by the elevators. I told the manager so no one would fall and get hurt. (I was really referring to myself). After we went to bed that night, Mandy began crying for her bottle. As I was filling it up, I dropped the carton of milk on the floor, spilling half of it.

All of these things happened after spending six hours in the car with three kids, two of whom fought off and on all the way—Robert and Rachel. Mandy, who I expected to be restless, was great. She just sat in her car seat all the way, drinking her bottle and dozing off occasionally. The only problem with her was she didn't like sleeping away from home. So I guess it almost evened out. Rachel and Robert were good at night, and Mandy was good during the day.

We went to SeaWorld the next day, and thankfully, all three kids behaved themselves. On our way home, we decided to see Lake Erie since we were so close. Well, we got on a toll road that I will have nightmares about the rest of my life. If you miss your exit, as we did, the next one is anywhere from twenty to thirty miles away. And there is no cutting across to go the other direction. After losing about an hour, we finally made it to Lake Erie. Eddie stayed home for this trip, and I think he was actually the one who had a vacation.

***

Another trip I made when my children were young was to Nashville, Indiana, where there are all kinds of unique little shops to explore. We had a nice time, but the trip wasn't without Sharon stories. First of all, I forgot that Indiana time was an hour behind ours. So when we arrived at ten in the morning our time, it was really only nine o'clock, and the shops were not yet open. Without thinking, we went inside the first little shop and started looking around. We didn't break in—the door was unlocked. The owner immediately showed us out and told us to come back in an hour. How embarrassing! Good thing the town was too small to have a post office; otherwise, our pictures may have been posted there. Plus, the beds at the hotel where we stayed made funny noises every time we sat on them. It sounded like we ate too many beans for dinner.

When our children were little, my sister and I took them to an "exotic animal farm" about an hour from my home. Everyone who worked there seemed to have an attitude, like they would rather be anywhere else. The exhibit was not very big, so it didn't take us long to see everything. And the most exotic animal I saw was a skunk from Indiana. On the way home, I managed to spill a malt. We stopped at a gas station so I could clean it off my clothes. We asked if they had a restroom, and they said they did. What they failed to tell us, though, was that the water was not working! Well, we didn't ask that, did we?

***

In 1997, when my daughters were eight and eleven, I took them to Myrtle Beach, South Carolina, with my friend, Debbie, and her two children. The first night of our trip, we stopped at a motel with our rented minivan and planned on arriving at the beach the next day. We woke up to a slashed tire. A man at our motel tried to pump it up with a portable compressor, but the air was coming out as fast as it was going in. So we drove it next door to a restaurant and walked back to a service garage that happened to be behind it. As it turned out, that garage was the only one authorized to do business on that property, and it had a cash-only policy. A man drove a tow truck over to the van, took off the tire, and went back to the garage to see how bad it was. The tire had to replaced. We lost three hours of travel time, plus I was out eighty-six dollars of my spending money.

We did make it to Myrtle Beach finally and had a great time. In fact, a five-dollar bill floated into Debbie's hand as we sat on the beach. The only thing that floated to me was a dead fish. At our last motel stop on our way home, Debbie made mention of an attic door that was in the ceiling of our room. She had me so scared that I slept with my shoes on my hands just in case there was trouble. I figured if someone did come in, and I jumped up with shoes on my hands, I would confuse them, if nothing else. I had no other way to protect myself. We all felt safe then, because Debbie slept with her son who knew karate, Rachel slept with Debbie's daughter who was a screamer, and I slept with Mandy with my trusty shoes on my hands.

***

Debbie and I also took our children to the Ohio State Fair in 1997. The trip was uneventful, except that when we first arrived in our motel, I couldn't find our toothbrushes, although I was sure I had packed them. After no luck in locating them, I spent $1.25 each on three new toothbrushes from a vending machine. I found the ones I'd brought from home after that. Oh well, no use being down in the mouth about it.

***

In 1998, I took a trip to Las Vegas with my coworker, Judy. This was the first time I had flown on a commercial flight. It was scary thinking about how high we were when we were flying over the Rocky Mountains. But then someone told me it's even scarier if you are getting really close to them.

When we arrived in Vegas, Judy and I were waiting for our luggage at the claims area. As we kept our eye on the conveyor, we noticed a badly damaged suitcase coming toward us. There were clothes hanging out of it everywhere, and it was obvious that the lid was no longer functional. It made several more trips around with no one coming forward to claim ownership. About the third time, I told Judy I felt sorry for whoever it belonged to. We waited there a little longer, and finally everyone had their luggage but me. The next time the damaged piece made its way to us, I took a closer look. It started looking familiar. Not because of the luggage itself, but I recognized the clothes that were hanging out of it. Yes, the destroyed suitcase was in fact mine. It was like that old Samsonite commercial where the ape jumped up and down on the luggage to show how sturdy it was. The problem was, mine was not Samsonite. And it looked like they had the ape jump on it anyway!

***

I had a very adventurous "weekend" trip in 1999. My sister invited her daughter and I to go with her to New York City while she attended a conference for a product she was selling. The company chartered a bus to take us from Cincinnati to our destination in New York. We were leaving on a Friday and supposed to return in the wee hours of Sunday morning. First of all, the bus was twenty-five minutes late meeting us. When it finally arrived, one of the first things I heard was from a fellow passenger asking, "Hey, did you notice that all the tires don't match?" That should have been a warning.

We had just started our journey when we made our first stop at a Meijer store. We later learned the reason for this stop was because the two drivers, who I later referred to as Dumb and Dumber, were getting directions. They thought we were going to Atlantic City. I was beginning to wonder if installing windows was their real occupation and driving buses was their side job. There was nothing professional about them. Once they finally figured out where to go, we noticed that the driver kept turning the air-conditioning on high. We got so cold that some of us bought blankets at one of the stops we made. Then a passenger began to complain about the stench in the back of the bus. Apparently, the toilet had not been emptied after the last trip, and it had backed up. The air-conditioner was the driver's way of trying to cover up the smell. Or at least freeze us to death so we would have other things to worry about. Eventually, we made a stop at a restaurant in Pennsylvania and were told to stay on the bus and not look out the windows as the driver made his way to the back lot. Well, of course, everyone looked. Our faces were plastered against the windows as we saw the toilet being dumped, illegally I am sure.

We continued on to New York City, where we arrived two hours late. Our guide was waiting for us, and we were taken to our hotel. The next morning my sister went to her conference. Her daughter and I decided to explore the city, and everyone was to meet back at the bus at four thirty. My niece and I knew we had to keep track of the time to make it back. We began walking and somehow ended up in a sort of bad part of the city where all the hot goods are sold. When we realized it, we turned around and headed back toward Times Square.

My niece was wearing her watch, and after walking a bit I asked her what time it was. She said it was two thirty, which meant we still had two hours before we had to meet the bus. Well, shortly after that I saw a big clock on one of the buildings, and it said 4:10 p.m. We then realized my niece's watch had stopped! We were panicked. We had to make a mad rush back to the bus at Thirty-Fourth and Sixth from where we were in Times Square, at Forty-Sixth and Eighth. Since it was our first time in New York and we just had that one day to explore, neither of us took the time to learn the bus and subway systems, so we had to make it back on foot. With the way the trip was going, it would be our luck that for once the bus would be on time. Somehow we made it back by four thirty, but it didn't matter. The bus was late anyway. When it arrived at five o'clock, we began the return trip home.

We were about one hour out of New York when the bus stalled in the middle of nowhere. Dumb and Dumber checked it out and said the engine was overheated, but we would be back on the road in fifteen minutes. Well, four hours and three police cars later, we were still on the side of the road. By now it was dark, and the emergency interior lights had gone out on the bus. Passengers were using their cell phones for light. Meanwhile, our drivers were trying to fix the bus via a telephone call with their supervisor, but they had no tools and no emergency equipment. All we had were a few florescent safety triangles that were left by one of the police officers who stopped earlier.

Finally, a Greyhound bus stopped for us and took us four miles to the nearest town. We went inside a coffee shop and waited. The driver at last informed us that there would be another bus coming at six in the morning to take us the rest of the way home. We were told to go to the hotel next door for the night. So the whole busload of passengers checked in and were given key cards for their rooms. My sister, my niece, and I were going to share one. Everyone was able to get into their rooms but us. So we went to the front desk, told them our problem, and were given a new key card. We got in this time, but when I turned on the light switch, there was a tiny puff of light, and then we were in the dark. We called the front desk and were informed that we could come and get some bulbs, but we would have to replace them ourselves because, as luck would have it, the maintenance man was off that night. So that's what we did.

In the morning, we waited for the new bus, which did not come at six as promised. In fact, it did not arrive until eleven thirty. We finally started on our way home with eleven hours of driving ahead of us. We made one last stop in Millville, Pennsylvania, to get dinner. This happened to be the same town where the toilet had been dumped. I was sitting at a table with my sister and niece, and they both got their drinks with no problem. Not me. Mine was spilled across the table. We began laughing, and the waiter thought we were laughing at him. But it was the whole weekend adventure that was so amusing. I did comment that at least we had good weather. We finished our dinner and then we all got back onto the bus.

I thought that had to be the end of our bad luck. I was mistaken. As we were leaving the parking lot, the back end of the bus got caught on the sloped driveway. We were stuck. Dumb and Dumber told everyone to vacate the bus, which we did. Somehow they managed to get us unstuck. Suddenly, as we were getting ready to board the bus again, we heard a clap of thunder, and the rain came. So much for the weather being good. Because of all the delays, the weekend trip turned into something else. We didn't get home until twelve thirty that Monday morning. I tried to tell everyone before the trip even started that I have bad luck and that weird things happen to me. They all said not worry, those things happen to everybody. Well, now they know. One of my favorite sayings is I'd rather get hit by a bus than ride one, and now I mean that more than ever.

***

In 2007, my sister and I took a bus tour to New York City to see the Macy's Thanksgiving Day parade. My seat number on the bus was thirteen, which was no surprise to me. Even though I am old, I enjoyed seeing the Energizer Bunny float up close. We also got to see the Rockettes Christmas show. Everyone in the audience was given little star lights to turn on toward the end of the show. Of course, mine did not work. Neither did the second one I was given. No one else appeared to have that problem.

***

A few years later, I went back to New York City with some lady friends. This was my third time there, and I was determined to finally go to the top of the Empire State Building. Since the other ladies didn't want to go, I ventured out on my own. I have found that most people in New York are as nice and helpful as can be, but there are exceptions to every rule. All of the buses have a sign posted near the driver that says, "Do not talk to the driver while the bus is in motion." I got on a bus headed for the Empire State Building, and it had the same sign, but with most of it crossed out. The only part left was "Do not talk to the driver." Period! I got the message.

I finally made it to the top of the Empire State Building, which was great. There is a mirrored wall where you can take your own picture and the New York City scenery will be behind you. Since I was alone, I thought that would be a good thing to do. So I took out my camera, which had dead batteries. I loaded in new ones—after first dropping them—held up my camera, and took my own picture. A normal person would have had the sense to hold the camera to the side. Not me! All that can be seen in the picture is a camera in front of a face and a flash. My kids got a kick out of that one. I think it explains why I had my own elevator on the way back down to the ground level.

***

In 2007, I decided to take my daughters on a cruise. Rachel was in college, and Mandy was a high school senior. We had to fly to New Orleans to meet our ship. My daughters had never flown before, and I had only flown a few times, so that was an adventure in itself. I thought I was going to have to pry Rachel's white-knuckled hands off the arms of the seat by the time we landed. It didn't help that we had a giant bolt roll down the aisle from the cockpit, and no one seemed concerned. I guess it wasn't a vital part of the plane, because we got to New Orleans safe and sound.

Our cruise was wonderful. We were especially looking forward to our scheduled massages. We were supposed to get them all at the same time, but the lady doing mine got sick, so I had to reschedule for two hours later. My massage lasted longer than the girls' did, and when I came out, Rachel and Mandy were both at the front desk asking about me. I have a poor sense of direction, and I guess they were worried that I was wondering around alone and unsupervised.

When we went to the breakfast buffet one morning, I was the only one who managed to get a carton of sour milk. Then at one of the sit-down dinners, Mandy ordered the mushrooms as an appetizer, but she did not eat them. I asked her why, and she said she didn't know they were going to be "sarinated." That made us laugh.

Lastly, I found out near the end of our week-long cruise that I had not been using body wash every day like I thought. I can explain. The Lever 2000 in the shower was clearly marked body wash, which I thought was the man's soap. I assumed the unmarked Dove sitting next to it was the lady's soap. It was actually shampoo. That's what I had been using all week. I guess I should have worn wearing my reading glasses in the shower so I could see the fine print on all the beauty products.

***

My sister and I went to Renfro Valley, Kentucky, over Memorial Day weekend in 2006 to see an Elvis impersonator. Renfro Valley is a very laid-back town, and a lot of older people go there to see the shows. Even though there was very little traffic, construction was underway for another lane on the main road. We didn't understand why. There was a better chance of being hit by a wheelchair than by a car. Plus there was a tunnel under the road for pedestrians to use to avoid any oncoming traffic.

My sister and I arrived at Renfro Valley early and were walking around when a lady walked past us and said, "You two look alike." Then she kept right on walking. Strange!

Later my sister and I decided to have lunch before the afternoon show. We entered the restaurant, and the hostess took us to our seats. She said she couldn't take our order but would send over the waitress. We were surprised when the same lady returned a few minutes later to take care of us.

We ate our lunch and relaxed awhile, and then we made our way to the theater. We wondered why there was no line getting in. We checked our tickets—we were an hour late! The show was already in progress when we made our way to our seats. The remaining part of the show was great, and I am sure the first half was just as wonderful. We were just glad we made it before Elvis left the building.

After the show, we left to come home and stopped to get gas. The first pump we pulled up to did not work. After getting gas, we stopped to eat, and then drove the rest of the way home. My sister took me to her house so I could get my vehicle. I transferred all my stuff over, and somehow I managed to drive off with my container of leftovers on top of my van. Once again, I don't do well in the adult role.

***

In 2007, I went back to Renfro Valley with some lady friends to see a gospel music show and a classic country music show. I drove, and as luck would have it, the air-conditioning in my van completely pooped out on the way there in the ninety-degree heat. So I had to have it fixed while there. It ended up just being low on coolant, thank goodness. We ate in a little restaurant right before we started the drive home, and as I was getting ready to leave, I discovered my knife had somehow fallen into my purse. I told the ladies teasingly that's how I replenish my silverware at home—I just take what I need when I am eating out.

***

Even when I go out of town to help others, I can't have a normal experience. Gordy and I went to Joplin, Missouri, in 2011 with seven others from our church to help with disaster relief after the tornado. We took our church van plus another truck. There was a church in Joplin that graciously allowed the many volunteers to sleep and eat there. We slept on air mattresses, and the men and women had separate rooms. We would start our day by having breakfast in the cafeteria. Each morning the men in our group would come in one by one and blame each other for the snoring that went on the night before. We never did figure out who the true guilty party was.

We spent a week helping to tear down what was left of the houses after the tornado. When everyone else was looking for sledgehammers and other heavy tools, I was swinging a mean lady's hammer. I know my own strength, which isn't that great.

One morning we stopped for breakfast on our way to the job site for that day. Unbeknownst to me, the truck had retractable running boards. I found out the hard way when I set my orange juice on one. The running boards went up, grabbed my juice, and dumped it before I could save it.

One day a few of us ladies helped stock the shelves with items for families affected by the tornado. My friend, Joy, and I were pulled from that task to a desk job in a nearby air-conditioned building. Not only were we in a cool environment, but we could have all the snacks and drinks we wanted. We even got a massage, which was being given to the volunteers. Whenever I began to feel bad knowing the rest of our group was out in the extreme heat, I would just have another pack of cookies, and somehow I felt better.

On another day we were given an easy job of breaking up huge bags of frozen lasagna and putting it in gallon-sized Ziploc bags. I almost broke my toe when I managed to drop one of the bags of frozen lasagna on my foot. My toe hurt for a whole day or two.

Something you wouldn't expect to see is a church van parked at a liquor store. But Gordy was out of cigarettes, it was late, and that was the only place we could find open. And it wasn't just any liquor store, but a discount liquor store. Our church van has huge letters on the side of it, so there was no hiding the fact we were there. We got in and out as quickly as possible.

I wondered why my back was damp every morning, and I didn't figure out why until the last day. It seems I was sleeping on the rubber side of the air mattress instead of the side with the nice material on it.

Not-So-Festive Festivals

Most people go to festivals and nothing strange or out of the ordinary ever happens. Not me! In 2007, I went to a festival in Kentucky, where I was meeting my family. By the time I got there, the only parking that was left looked like it was on the side of a mountain. After parking where I was directed by the attendant, I was afraid of getting stuck. My vehicle was at a steep angle, and there were ruts and tree roots everywhere. I expressed these concerns to the parking staff and was assured that I would have no problem getting out. I took them at their word, met up with my family, and enjoyed the festival. When it was time to leave, I began the long walk to my vehicle. Going back up the hill took a lot longer than going down, but I finally made it and was looking forward to getting home. When I tried to drive out of the parking area, however, my worst nightmare came to life—I was stuck! After several failed attempts to free my vehicle, I gave up and walked back down the hill to get help. I found the security personnel and they, in turn, called a tow truck. It took awhile, but I finally got out of the rut I was in.

***

Gordy and I like to go to canal days in Metamora, Indiana. It's a sleepy little town, except for twice a year, when they have extra vendors come in for this event. I have been going to this for many years. Usually it's just a fun time eating and seeing all the crafts. During our visit in 2009, however, this was not the case. We had just paid for our lunch when the violence erupted. We witnessed a guy in a truck driving through the streets and another guy running after him, trying to fight. The streets are closed to traffic during canal days, so this was quite unusual. Since the streets were so crowded with people, the guy running was able to catch up to the truck, and a fistfight started through the open window. Meanwhile, the guy in the truck continued to drive through the crowd. All Gordy and I were trying to do was eat our lunch. We never thought we would have a front-row seat to a street brawl! Finally security came, and the truck drove off.

***

In the summer of 2013, my sister and I wanted to go a festival about twenty miles from my home. The hours were to be from two in the afternoon to ten o'clock at night, with crafts, food, music, and fireworks. We got there about two thirty, and absolutely nothing was going on. We asked one of the workers about it, and he said to get our friends and come back a little later when everything was set up. He promised it would be worth it. Instead of driving all the way back home, we went to a little nearby town and went through some of the shops. We did that until we were kicked out at five o'clock, when everything closed for the day. It must be a small town thing. So we went back to the festival, thinking it would be in full swing by then. Boy, were we wrong! The only music we heard was coming from a loud boom box, there was one funnel cake stand, and there were no crafters. There were about twenty people there total—including the vendors! I guess as long as there is one funnel cake and/or hot dog, it is considered a festival. We asked someone where the crafters were, and they said there were supposed to be crafters, but no one wanted to do it. Needless to say, we were disappointed. So we came back home and ended up going to a festival less than a mile from my house.

Yard Sales

Yard sales can be a pain. At one of mine, I had a car full of teenagers do a drive-by and yell-by. As they passed, I heard, "Got any good stuff? It doesn't look like it." At that same yard sale, a man on a motorcycle bought my baby crib. I'm not sure how he got it home.

When my girls were small, we had a yard sale, and they were so excited. They thought for sure we were going to be rich and were already making plans on how to spend all the money. We ended up making about four dollars, and most of that was because of their lemonade sales.

There is always something that is in a yard sale that you are desperate to get rid of so you don't have to drag it back in the house. For me, it was my old Christmas tree. I started telling potential customers to take the tree or they were getting a kitten. It didn't work, but it was worth a try!

Restaurant Woes

It's hard for me to have a normal restaurant experience. When I was pregnant with my third child, I went to lunch by myself one day. While waiting for the hostess to seat me, other people joined me in line. Assuming I was with the man standing behind me, the hostess said, "Table for two?" Looking down toward my stomach, I replied, "Not yet."

Another time I had the opposite happen when I was with two other ladies. The hostess came over and looked right at those two and said, "Table for two?" I said, "No, table for three. I am with them." And she said, "Oh, I didn't even see you."

My friend, Terri, and I went to lunch one day, and we had just sat down at our booth. All of a sudden, the tiny lights on the wall next to our booth started sparking and crackling. We noticed that no one else near us was experiencing that. I wasn't surprised.

I was walking into a Wendy's restaurant one time and a customer coming out handed me some coupons, which I thought was nice. That's until I noticed that the coupons were expired.

One time I was questioned about my lunch order at a Roy Rogers restaurant. I waited by the counter while my order was filled. When my food never came, I inquired about it. I was asked what I ordered, and when I told them, they basically told me that I was wrong. Wouldn't I be the one to know?

I went to a sports bar for lunch with some coworkers. A few of them ordered appetizers, but I just wanted pretzels. What I got was a crab cake. That's close. Once again, no one listens to me.

I went to lunch with some coworkers one day. As everyone was placing their orders, several of them asked what came on this and what came on that. I ordered a grilled cheese, and I asked what came on it. Everyone laughed, but with the way my luck is, I figured I had better ask.

Getting ignored in restaurants is what I do best. I feel like they put me in the noneating section because a lot of times I don't get the basics like water, silverware, or food. It's like once I step into a restaurant, I become invisible. Even if I am lucky enough to get seated, that is the last sign of life I see. It doesn't matter if I'm by myself or with others.

***

One time I went to lunch with about eight coworkers. We were seated, and the waiter came over to take our orders. After a bit, everyone's food was brought out—everyone's, that is, except mine. I waited patiently until the waiter asked if everything was okay or if we needed anything. That's when I told him I didn't get my food.

He looked at me like I was from Mars and said, "Well, how long have you been here? Did you just arrive?"

I said, "No, I came in with everyone else."

He looked at me like saying, *Yeah, right.* He did take my order (again), and I got to watch everyone else eat until I finally got my lunch.

***

I went to Bob Evans one day on my lunch hour from work, and I happened to be wearing a red-and-white checked dress. Unfortunately for me, the uniforms of the waitresses and hostess at that time were also red-and-white checked dresses. I sat and sat, waiting on someone to take my order. The only reason I can think of as to why I was ignored is that they thought I was an employee on break or something. In addition, whenever I wore that dress to work, one of my coworkers would jokingly call my line and order breakfast.

I was with four other people when we went to lunch one day. Everyone got their food, drinks, etc., except for me. I didn't even have any silverware. The waitress returned and said, "Is everything okay here?" I told her no, it wasn't. Everyone else was eating, and I didn't have anything. Not even a glass of water. She replied, "Oh, I'm sorry. I forgot yours."

One afternoon I stopped for lunch at a little local restaurant. When my order was brought to me, it wasn't quite right. I told the waitress I believed my lunch was switched with someone else's. She took my food, went to another table, and made the switch, which was kind of gross. The other diner and I had both already touched our chips. I lost my appetite after that.

At another restaurant I was asked if I wanted breakfast or lunch. Even though I said breakfast, I was given the lunch menu. After I got that straightened out, I placed my order. My food came, but my drink never did. When I finally got the waitress to bring it, she said, "Sorry. I forgot all about you." Then when I went to pay my bill, I was shortchanged. Just a regular restaurant experience for me.

***

One evening in August 2007, I went to dinner with my friend, Dee, to a new Italian restaurant I was excited to try. The waitress brought us our menus. Dee placed her order, and I decided on the lasagna. About five minutes later, the cook came over, looked straight at me, and said, "I'm sorry, we are out of lasagna." He went on to say that it would take about forty-five minutes to prepare, so if I wanted to order something else, they would give both me and my friend lasagna to take home because of the inconvenience. So I went ahead and ordered something else.

A little while later, the waitress came over and apologized again for being out of lasagna and said that they were going to give us each a free dessert to make up for it. So our meals came, we ate our dinner, and then the waitress brought us the dessert menus. Once again, my friend ordered hers, and I ordered mine. The waitress left then returned five minutes later, looked straight at me, and said, "I am sorry, we are out of the dessert you wanted." She went on to say that she and the cook were debating on who should relay the bad news to me for the second time. The cook told the waitress she had to do it since he was the bearer of the bad news the first time around. All I could do was laugh. The waitress commented on how well I was taking the situation, and I explained to her that this is just how my luck is. If I got upset every time I got the wrong food or no food in a restaurant, I would never go out to eat. But it all worked out. My friend and I got free lasagna and free dessert. Maybe when I go to a restaurant, I should just save time and ask what they are out of, because that is what I want.

***

My next adventure happened when I stopped in a hamburger place to get a quick lunch. It turned into one bad event after another. I was ignored, which I should have been used to by then. It took forever to get a seat, even though I was the only person in line. After that was finally accomplished, it took a good ten minutes for the waitress to come and take my order. Then, it took a long time to get my food.

A family was brought over to sit near my table. I didn't mind until the four-year-old child started having a fit and began kicking. Since we shared the same long bench seat that was along the outer wall of the restaurant, that meant the boy was kicking me. Finally, after my glaring at the parents, the child stopped and kept his feet on his side of the bench.

Once that was over, I finished my food and was ready to leave. But it took a long time the get my bill. While I was waiting on that, I decided to fill out one of the comment cards that were on the table to let the restaurant know that I was not pleased with the service I had received. So I found a pen in my purse (an accomplishment in itself) and began to fill out the card. To my shock, I noticed my hand was all blue—not because it was cold, but because my pen had sprung a very bad leak. I had quite a mess when the waitress finally returned. Could anything else go wrong? Well, yes, it could. To complete my visit, I managed to spill my drink on some papers I was going over for work. Just a typical day of eating out for me.

***

My daughter, Mandy, and I decided to stop for lunch at a little restaurant in Kentucky one day. We felt lucky that we got seated right away, but we realized the hostess had an attitude when she literally threw our menus on the table. It took awhile, but a waitress finally came to our table. After a long wait for our food, she returned and told us our order had been lost and she would have to take it again. When we finally did get our food, Mandy got mine, and I got hers. Also, Mandy never got the refill on her drink that

94

she requested. When we got our bill, we discovered I was overcharged for the lunch special, which made it a little less special. As the correction was being made, I told the waitress I would like to have a piece of cheesecake to go. The next thing I saw was cheesecake on a plate with two forks. When I told the waitress we wanted to take it with us, she put it in a to-go box. On the drive home, we got behind a vehicle that had fire coming out of the back of it. (It must have been a Blazer.) My luck continued: we got back to Mandy's apartment, opened the container, and found that the cheesecake had been put in the box upside down.

Maybe I just shouldn't order desserts to go. One time when I got home with my piece of strawberry pie, I opened the box, and it looked like it had been hit by a bus. With my luck, it probably had been.

I have had Bob Evans run out of milk, our local deli run out of bread, and Kentucky Fried Chicken run out of chicken (what am I supposed to order when that happens?) Also on one of my visits to the United Dairy Farmers, the only flavor of ice cream they were out of was cookies and cream—the one I wanted. On another visit, they were out of orange drink for the freeze that I ordered. I went to eat at a steakhouse, and they were out of the cut of meat that I like. One time I even had a fortune cookie with no fortune inside.

I went out to breakfast with my husband one time and ordered eggs over easy and crispy bacon. What I got was scrambled eggs and wimpy bacon. Another time, I was the only one at our table who got a small glass of water—even though there were children with us. I have also been cut off at a drive-through by a walk-up! Once I was asked if I wanted sauce with my chicken pieces and I said, "Yes, honey." But I guess they thought I meant "Yes, Honey," because I got a weird look. I had to say it a different way for them to know I wanted honey with my chicken and I wasn't getting personal with anyone.

One time I went through the McDonald's drive-through and ordered a fish sandwich with cheese. Something happened to my words between the speaker and the restaurant because I wasn't being understood. I was asked to repeat my order, which I did. I was asked to repeat it again, which I did. With the third request, I lost my patience and raised my voice considerably.

There was silence and then I heard, "All right," in a loud voice right back to me. When I got to the window to get my food, I apologized for my actions but told them they might as well just have a hole where the speaker was because it wasn't working anyway. I think the cashier agreed.

I was getting ice cream out of a soft-serve machine when a feather appeared. I guess it really was soft serve.

Years ago I went a revolving restaurant, set my purse inside the rail by the window, and had to wait for it to come back to me.

I got a carry-out dinner for my family from Kentucky Fried Chicken one night. I was supposed to get mashed potatoes, green beans, slaw, and of course, chicken. What I got was two orders of mashed potatoes, french fries, slaw, and not one piece of chicken. Did I look like a vegetarian? Earlier this same day, Subway had run out of drinks and chips for the combo meals I wanted.

Gordy and I went to lunch at a fast-food restaurant, and I ordered a cheeseburger, fries, and a small Frosty. Well, I got no fries, and the Frosty I got was the kid's size. It had about two spoons of ice cream in it. Of course, Gordy's order was exactly as he had ordered it.

Gordy and I ate at Bobby Flay's one afternoon. I was sitting at the counter eating my hamburger when a guy carrying a tray of sauce bottles came by me. Wouldn't you know it—he dropped the whole tray on the floor right next to me, and one of the bottles began squirting right on my pant leg.

The following lunch related stories all happened within four days. The first one happened on a Tuesday, when I ordered the double cheeseburger special at a fast-food restaurant. The cashier said she wasn't sure how to ring it up, but she would check and be right back. Sure she would. She didn't return for a good three minutes, and then she began taking care of other customers. When I asked her if she was going to ring up my order she said, "Oh, I'm sorry. I forgot all about you." The next day at work we placed a large order for some cheese Coneys and chili three-ways to be picked up for lunch. Of course, mine was the only order out of the fifteen that wasn't in the bag. On that Friday, I stopped at Long John Silver's for lunch and ordered a fish dinner. The cashier saw me get the vinegar sauce for it and told me it would be a few minutes. She said I should just take a seat and she would bring it out. Well, what she brought out looked a little "fishy." I took a bite of it, and it turned out to be chicken.

It was a Sunday night when I stopped to get tacos for my family. After waiting in the drive-through for what seemed like forever, I decided that I had waited long enough. I mean, it's either a hard shell or a soft shell. How hard can it be? So I got out of the drive-through line, parked my car, and stormed into the restaurant, up to the front of the line. Surprisingly, no one stopped me. I guess they knew I was a woman on a mission. I told the cashier I had been waiting in the drive-through line a good twenty minutes, and I wanted my tacos. After all, I said, my kids had school in the morning, and I wanted them to eat before that. Without another word, my ordered was completed, and I came out carrying my box of tacos. Everyone who was still in line began honking their horns and waving at me. It was a good feeling.

***

Sometimes instead of food issues, I have silverware issues. One time I went to Red Lobster with my family and noticed that my wrapped silverware was heavier than everyone else's. I guess I should have been happy that I got some at all, knowing my luck. I unwrapped it and discovered why it was so heavy. It seems that instead of a normal spoon, mine was a huge serving spoon.

When my daughter, Rachel, turned twenty-one, I took her out to eat to celebrate. We both got linen-wrapped silverware, but when I opened mine, the utensils looked like they had been used to cut a piece of double-chocolate cake, and the napkin looked like it was used to clean up the mess! Rachel, of course, did not have this problem.

I am a slow eater. I was out to dinner with my family one time, and I was the only one still eating when the waitress came over to check on us. When she noticed all the food I still had on my plate she said, "What's wrong, didn't you like your food?" And I said, "No, I just eat slow." I think the word is out, because at a different restaurant I unwrapped my silverware and instead of the usual knife, fork, and spoon, I got three forks. Maybe that's so I eat faster?

***

Sometimes I am just the victim of the bizarre. Years ago I was taking my children out to eat, and as we were driving to the restaurant, we saw a bird fly in front of my van. We never saw it again, so we assumed it flew off. After dinner, I drove home and pulled my van into the garage. Rachel walked around to the front of the van and said, "Mom, you have to see this." The bird we had seen earlier was stuck in the grille of my van with its wings spread out like he was in flight. I thought about where we parked at the restaurant and was glad that we did not park facing it. I knew if we did, no one would want to order the chicken.

Food Troubles at Home

By now it's clear that eating out has its issues for me. Staying home is not much better. I have had spaghetti sauce spilled into my shoes and pop spilled into my purse. I also dropped a box of fettuccine on the floor, and when it landed on its end, the pasta jumped out of the box like fireworks. You can put an eye out that way.

One time when my son was little, I was making a cake to take to work. He was watching me at the kitchen counter while playing with a pen. I just got the cake batter into the big pan to put in the oven when I noticed the top of the pen was no longer in sight. After checking around the work space and the floor and not finding it, I thought it may have fallen into the cake batter. It would have been almost impossible to dump the cake batter back out of that big pan, so I sifted through it with a fork, hoping to find the missing top, with no luck. I finally decided to bake the cake and hope for the best. I did not detect any melting plastic, so I took the cake to work. It was fine, thank goodness, but I never found the pen top. Weird.

For a special event, I made a cake for my daughter's Girl Scout troop. To decorate it, I made a pattern out of paper by folding it and cutting it so it looked like girls holding hands when it was laid on the cake. Then I sprinkled all around it with powdered sugar and removed the paper pattern. I also decorated the edge of the cake with a border. Our Girl Scout meeting was canceled that night because of bad weather. When we had the meeting the next night, I got quite a surprise when I uncovered the cake. Overnight, the powdered sugar had been absorbed, and the only thing left was the border. We ate the cake anyway.

Sharon Who?

Not only am I ignored in restaurants, it happens in other situations too. When I worked downtown, I was waiting on the corner to be picked up for lunch. It was a gray day, and I had on a gray coat. I saw my ride pull up to a traffic light. When the light turned green, I stepped closer to the curb and watched as the car continued on past me. The driver circled the block and then stopped to pick me up.

She asked me, "Hey, why weren't you waiting for me. I had to go around the block."

I replied, "I was here, and you just passed me up."

"Oh, I thought you were a lump of cement," she explained.

"Does a lump of cement do this?" I asked, waving my arms.

***

When I was playing the *Wheel of Fortune* video game one time, I was totally skipped when it was my turn. How is that even possible?

I was at a class for work on how to be more assertive when this next incident occurred. There were about twenty of us sitting at a big table, and the facilitator divided us into two groups. He said everyone to the left of me would be in one group and everyone to my right would be in another. That left me in no group. When I raised my hand (assertively, of course) and told him, he said he was sorry, he didn't see me.

I went to another meeting for work and my name wasn't even on the attendance sheet.

More Bad Luck

Shortly after I moved into my house in 1988, I received an application in the mail for a new credit card. Upon receipt of the completed paperwork, applicants were to get a free gift—a pair of sunglasses. One part of the application asked for present and previous address, which I included. I filled out the application and sent it in. A week or so later, I was notified that I did not qualify for the credit card because I had not lived in my current residence long enough. I still received the glasses, but to add insult to injury, one of the arms was missing. I guess that's what the credit card rejects got.

***

My daughters had a day off school one day in 2000 and I decided to take them to the museum center in Cincinnati. My son, who was an adult and living in Northern Kentucky, also wanted to go. So I picked Robert up on the way and then I stopped to get gas at a station on the opposite side of the street. I didn't want a fill-up—just enough to insure I would not run out, since I was a fair distance from home. I got my five dollars' worth of gas and crossed the road to continue on to my destination.

I wasn't on the road two minutes when I noticed a police car behind me with his siren and lights going. I thought, *Oh, no. What did I do wrong?* I pulled over and waited for the policeman to walk up to my driver's side window. He asked me if I knew why I was being pulled over. I told him I did not. He then asked me if I had just gotten gas. I told him I did. Then he said it was reported that someone in a blue van like mine had pumped gas, threw the pump on the ground, and drove off without paying. I told him that was absolutely not me. First of all, if I really wanted to steal gas, I wouldn't have stopped at five dollars, I would have gotten a fill-up. And I certainly wouldn't have chosen a gas station that was so close to police headquarters, and where I had to cross traffic for my getaway. Also I didn't have to come to Kentucky to start my life of crime, as there were plenty of gas stations to hit in my own state of Ohio. And I certainly wouldn't have my children in the vehicle to witness my criminal act. These arguments did not change the policeman's mind. In fact, he insisted on not only running my license through the system, but also that of my son, who was in the passenger seat.

By this time, a second officer had arrived. He didn't believe my story either, and unfortunately I had not gotten a receipt for the gas. I kept pleading my case, but to no avail. One of the officers told me I would have to go to court and bring my witnesses, which I guess meant my children, two of whom were minors. Finally, a third police car pulled up, and I saw the officer from that vehicle talk to the other two. The next thing I knew, one of them came up to my window and informed me that there had been a mistake. It was another person driving another blue van that had stolen the gas. Really! Wasn't that's what I had been trying to tell them for the last fifteen minutes? I was so glad the ordeal was over and I didn't end up on the eleven o'clock news.

***

I don't think I have a suspicious-looking face, but I must be wrong. After the gas station incident, I bought some fruit from a little fruit stand, paid with a twenty-dollar bill, and watched as it was scrutinized by not just one cashier, but two. It was held up to the light, and the two ladies whispered between themselves before finally deciding it was real. Once again, if I were going to steal, I would make the most of it and not stop at two apples and a couple of bananas.

Sometimes at work, employees would be randomly drug tested. Some people never got to experience this, but it happened to me three times. I can barely swallow an aspirin when I need it, much less take something illegal. When my name came up for the third time, my supervisor was almost afraid to tell me, since I had nearly lost it the second time it happened. I wondered how it was possible for my name to come up three times for that, but I don't have any luck winning anything. The only item I ever won in my life was a beautifully engraved cigarette lighter. Unfortunately, I don't smoke.

***

101

Grocery shopping has never been on my list of favorite things to do. Here is just one reason why. I was perfectly happy waiting for my turn at the checkout one day when a cashier waved me over to her newly opened line. I was glad to have this opportunity to get out of the store quicker. Well, first she couldn't get the register to open. Then after I had half my groceries unloaded, the scanner wouldn't work, so she was going to have to enter all the numbers by hand. Since that was going to take forever, she asked me to pack up the groceries and move to the other line, which happened to be the one where I started. Except now the line was longer. Sometimes maybe it's better to get ignored. If she hadn't seen me waiting, I probably would have been out of the store fifteen minutes sooner.

Other not-so-pleasant experiences include having my credit card sucked up into the conveyor belt, a can of biscuits explode while checking out, a can of whipped cream explode in my car, and a watermelon roll out of the back of my vehicle and split in two.

One time during a storm, a power outage occurred while I was doing my grocery shopping. As soon as the store went totally dark, I heard screaming. Then I realized it was me. What can I say? It was scary!

When I go grocery shopping, I just want to get it over with. But sometimes I get involved in the lives of other customers. I have had strangers ask my opinion on which diapers are best (even though my children have been out of them for years and years), which marinade I would recommend, and where to find the ground red pepper. I also had a customer ask me to watch her baby for a minute. Do I look like I work there?

Gordy and I went to the grocery store recently and were shocked when our three small bags added up to seventy-nine dollars. I went ahead and paid the bill, and then we checked our receipt. I wondered just how good that melon was going to be when I noticed we were charged thirty-eight dollars for it!

***

Mandy got me a cute pair of stylish boots for Christmas one year. I waited for the perfect time to wear them, and that day came. I put them on and went into my kitchen. As I was walking, I saw something brown roll across the piece of carpet under my kitchen table. As my luck would have it, the toe of my brand-new boots had made contact with a "deposit" from my dog, who happened to have a rare accident that same day. My daughter tells me all the time I have the worst luck ever. I think I do.

Uncoordinated "R" Me

I never was athletic. In fact, when I was in gym class at school, I was always the last one chosen for any sort of team. If it came down to me and a person in a body cast, I am pretty sure that person would have been chosen first. It didn't change once I was an adult, either.

***

Despite my lack of gymnastic ability, I decided take my seven-year-old son skiing for the first time at Perfect North Slopes in Indiana. I thought it was nice that we were offered breakage insurance in case we broke an arm or a leg. Little did I know. They told me the insurance was for their equipment—not bones.

I learned a few other things too. I learned that the hardest thing about skiing is grabbing on to that rope that takes you to the top of the beginner hill. If it's not done just right, it feels like your arm is being ripped out of the socket as you are dragged to the top. And don't fall, because no one can help. They are just learning too. When I fell, a man came over and asked if I was all right. I said, "No, I need some help getting up." He said, "Okay" and skied off. It's hard trying to stand back up on those long skis once you have fallen, but somehow I did it.

My son, of course, had no trouble with the beginner hill. Kids are like that. They just seem to catch on to things sooner than us old folks. Finally, after some practice, I felt comfortable enough to try the intermediate hill. This has to be reached by chair lift. After reaching the top, I found out there is a right and wrong way to get out of the chair. I chose the wrong way and found myself skiing sooner than I wanted to—and I was going backward. Fortunately, I managed to get myself turned around the right way. When skiing down the hill, no one told me to go back and forth. So I went straight down. Bad idea. By the time I got to the bottom, I felt like I was breaking the land-speed record. I could almost see those frightened faces of the people in the lodge at the bottom of the hill as I was fast approaching. Fortunately, someone opened the door at the last minute, so I didn't have to make my own new entrance.

***

There have been a few times in my life, though, that I surprised myself with my athletic movements. Like the morning I had just gotten up and noticed a bee buzzing around my overhead light in the kitchen. I found a fly swatter and proceed to swing at the bee. As my luck would have it, when I hit the bee, it fell straight down my nightgown. In my panic, I did some moves that would make an Olympic gymnastics champion proud. Finally, my daughter said the bee was on the floor, and I could stop being a contortionist.

Then there was the time when I was cutting my grass, and I ran over a ground hornet's nest. I didn't know a person (especially me) could run and strip at the same time, but that's exactly what I did as I made my way into my house. By the time I made it inside, I was missing a few pieces of clothing, but I also missed getting a few more bee stings.

When my girls were young, we got new carpet in our living room, and our family was enjoying some snacks while watching TV. I don't know why, but we were drinking red Kool-Aid. You would think it would be the kids to worry about spilling the drink on the new carpet, but it was me—the adult. I got up from the couch and tripped over the dog while I was carrying the last of my Kool-Aid to the kitchen. I was stumbling around trying to regain my balance, and the drink was sloshing around in the glass. In the back of my mind, I told myself no matter what, I couldn't let that red stuff hit my carpet. It seemed like it took forever, but believe it or not, I made it to the kitchen without spilling a drop. I surprised even me.

Bad Days

Everyone has a bad day now and then. I have had my share of them. On one such day, I fell down some steps at work and ended up with a big, giant bruise on my rear. I was too embarrassed to go to the doctor. That same day I was going through the drive-through at Taco Bell, which was very long. I was just cruising along behind the car in front of me when I realized I had passed up the speaker where I was supposed to place my order.

I took my kids to a horse show at an arena in Alexandria, Kentucky one afternoon. While we were sitting in the stands, a girl was walking up the steps, lost her balance, and collapsed onto me. Then, as we were leaving after the show, my purse somehow got hooked on a lawn chair someone had in the stands and I ended up dragging it down a crowded aisle. If that wasn't enough, I got ice cream cones for everyone, and after taking one lick off mine, the rest fell on the ground.

When my daughters were little, I helped out during Vacation Bible School. In just a few days' time, I managed to hit my chin, get kicked in the head, be pushed off a pew, and lose my balance during snack time, which resulted in dropping a cupcake while I slid down the wall. To top it all off, Mandy got sick and vomited one evening, and we ended up taking home someone else's craft. Looks like I'm not safe anywhere.

***

Another typical bad day started out with my not being able to lift the garage door because one of the wheels had come off the track. With the help of my ten-year-old daughter, we finally managed to get the problem resolved. That was just the start of my troubles that day. It was pouring down rain, and my coworker, Amy, and I were scheduled to deliver Meals on Wheels during our lunch hour. One of our clients lived under a funeral home, and it usually took her a few minutes to get to the door. I knocked and waited. Suddenly the door flew open, and we saw a man pushing a gurney. Fortunately, the lady we were waiting on wasn't on the gurney, but Amy said I should have seen the look on my face.

Later that afternoon, I took off early from work for a dentist appointment that I had set up the day before to get a crown started on my tooth. I had received a call stating they had a cancellation, and I was able to get in at the last minute. Apparently, someone important didn't get that message, because what I found when I arrived was the office completely closed for the day. There wasn't anything I could do about it, so I returned to work.

That evening an appraiser was scheduled to look at my house for a home equity loan. He called to say he was stuck in traffic on the other side of town and wanted to make it another time. Then last, but not least, my sister and I went to the new Meijer store at nine thirty at night to do our grocery shopping. When paying for my items, I wrote a check and, for some reason, the cash register refused to print the necessary information on it. The cashier had to call the manager. They said they had never had that problem before.

***

In 2010, Mandy invited me to go to the casino with her and a few of her friends. I was the only old person in the group. They all had better luck than I did. In fact, my luck was so bad I somehow managed to spill my soft drink all over my shoe. Then when I went to the restroom, I used the only sink where the soap dispenser didn't work.

***

In 2012, I wanted to refinance my house, and I met with the agent at the bank. He entered my information in the computer as I sat there in his office. Once he completed all the data, he tried to access it to recheck everything. Somehow it was lost in cyberspace and could not be retrieved. Since the bank was located in the front part of the grocery store, the agent suggested I do some shopping while he tried to straighten out the problem. I did just that. Just about the time I approached the check-out counter with my items, the cashier walked away without even noticing me. After finally getting done with that, I went back to the bank. The agent was still not able to retrieve my information. He told me to go home, and he would get back to me. After three days went by with no luck, he decided to resubmit the information. He told me that every now and then, there is a glitch in the computer system, but never to this extreme.

This same day, I was at home attempting to open a can of soup that had a pull tab. Unfortunately, when I pulled it, the tab came off in my hand. I tried to use the can opener on it, but that idea proved unsuccessful. Since I was in the middle of a recipe that needed the soup, my only option was plan B. This entailed jabbing the can with the point of the handheld can opener and making a hole big enough to shake out the soup. This took awhile, but I finally did it. After that, I took a pie crust out of my freezer. When I opened the package, it disintegrated into pieces. It must have been a full moon the night before, or maybe it was just my usual bad luck.

***

One evening, I used my Crock-Pot, washed it, and set it on my stove to dry. The next morning, I got up, made some cinnamon rolls, and used the cookie sheet they were on to move the Crock-Pot over when I got them out of the oven. Mandy, Gordy, and I were eating the rolls when Gordy said, "I smell something burning." He went into the kitchen and found one of my Crock-Pot legs burnt halfway down, along with the electric cord. Apparently, the cookie sheet pushed the Crock-Pot, and the control knob hit and pushed in the knob on the stove, causing the burner to turn on. We got out a fan to get the fumes from the plastic out of the kitchen.

A few minutes later, as I was getting off the couch, the recliner part came up just as I was passing and knocked me to the floor. I got up, went into the kitchen, and managed to knock the fan off the counter. As if that weren't enough, I noticed the water pump was running, even though no one was using water. Well, after checking the cistern, I found we were just about out of water, so we had to order some. All of this happened before ten in the morning. It was a Friday, but not Friday the thirteenth, like it seemed. Mandy said if she were me, she would never leave the house. But I said I wanted to leave the house. That was where everything bad was happening.

No One Listens to Me

Years ago I asked for my hair to be cut like Dorothy Hamill's, the female ice skater. What I got was a haircut like Mark Hamill's, the male actor. So I had to act as if I liked it until it grew out.

When my children were little, we took them to an amusement park. I was pulling them through the crowd in a wagon. There were a woman and some children not moving but just talking, and I was wanting to get through. I politely said "Excuse me" several times, with no response. Finally the lady turned around, saw me, and said to her kids, "Let this rude lady through. She doesn't even know how to say excuse me." Like I said, no one listens to me.

Recently my friend, Debi, wanted me to put her husband on our prayer list at church because he had a kidney stone he was having trouble passing, and he was in pain. I passed the information along via e-mail, but when it was retyped to put in the list of prayer requests for our church bulletin, something was missed. The name was correct, but it said he was having trouble passing a kidney. Wow! That *would* hurt.

What Was I Thinking?

Sometimes I think my brain goes on vacation without me. I was still half asleep when I glanced at the clock and immediately alerted my husband in a sort of panic. "Wake up," I said. "You're going to be late for work. The big hand is on the twelve and the little hand is one the six."

My husband jumped up out of bed and got about half dressed before he said, "Wait a minute. We have a digital clock!"

***

I was cleaning the surface of my kitchen appliances one day, and I reached under the sink for my stovetop cleaner. What I really grabbed was my dog's flea shampoo. I didn't realize my mistake until I had poured it out on my stove. Maybe that's why I don't like to clean—it always gets me in trouble.

Even when I try to be prepared for work there are problems. There was the time I put the TV remote in my purse instead of my glasses. That was an interesting day.

I even have issues when I pack my own lunch for work. There were two little bags on my kitchen counter one morning, and I grabbed the wrong one. I had quite a surprise at lunchtime that day when I opened it and found spices instead of my sandwich. I just can't trust me to get it right.

Years ago, when I worked downtown for Duke Energy, I used to park in a parking garage and walk to our building. Near the crosswalk, there was a sign on a post that said, "Caution, watch for traffic." It should have said, "Caution, watch for sign," because I walked right into it.

Once I drove all the way home from work, thought it was awfully quiet in the car, and then realized I forgot to pick up the kids from the babysitter's.

I was at work one day when it began to rain. The office at that time was in a one-floor building, and I could see my car in the parking lot. My car windows were down, so I ran out to wind them up. They weren't electric windows, so I had to do it by hand. I got the driver's side window up then ran around to the passenger side. That door was locked, so I ran into the office to get my key. I didn't even think about reaching over from the driver's side.

In 2004, both my daughters were working as waitresses at two different restaurants. Eddie and I had eaten at the one where Mandy worked several times and left her a nice tip. I told him that we needed to go to Bob Evans and do the same for Rachel. So one evening Mandy, Eddie, and I met at Bob Evans at Eastgate, about fifteen minutes from our home. My daughter had mentioned that there were three Rachels that worked the same shift, and we needed to make sure we were put in her serving area. When we requested that section, we got a surprise. We were told not only was there no Rachel Witherington that worked there, but they didn't have any Rachels working that shift. Well, we didn't know what to think at that point, since Mandy, Eddie and I all thought we were at the right place. I was wondering where Rachel went in her uniform if she wasn't going to work. We went ahead and ate, and I decided to ask Rachel about it later. As it turned out, she worked at the Bob Evans in Milford, which was the other direction from our home. She used to work at the Eastgate Frisch's, so I must have gotten the two mixed up. I felt pretty bad not knowing where my own daughter was working. I did feel better knowing I wasn't the only one mixed up about it.

Several years ago, Rachel was dropping off her vehicle to have some work done, and I was meeting her there. When I arrived at the garage, I asked the mechanic if she was there yet. He asked me what kind of vehicle she had, and I told him an Excalibur. He said, "Excalibur?" I told him I was sure that's what it was. About that time, Rachel arrived, and it was not an Excalibur she was driving, but an Equinox. It is a sharp-looking vehicle. Maybe that's why I got confused.

We were making steaks on the grill one evening, and I used the meat thermometer to make sure they were done to our preference. When I checked them for the last time, I wasn't sure what to do with the thermometer so I could carry in the steaks. I decided to stick it in my pocket. Not a good idea. Not only were the steaks at a hot temperature, but then my shorts were, too!

I don't even have a normal experience when I interact with my pets. One day I was playing with my dog, Snickers, and was trying to get the ball out of her mouth. When she finally let go, my arm flew back, and I hit myself in the face.

Then there was the time I took my dogs for a walk at our local park. I locked my van with the key clicker and took the dogs around the lake a few times. Then I returned to my van and discovered that the unlock function on the clicker would not work. I was in a panic, wondering how I was going to get home with my two dogs. I stood there for a good two or three minutes until the light finally came on in my mind—in addition to the clicker, I also had the key to the van in my hand.

On the day of Mandy's college graduation in 2013, she asked to drive my car because hers was acting funny. So she left a little early with my vehicle, and the rest of us went in Rachel's vehicle. After the ceremony, Mandy was going to follow us to the Cheesecake Factory. As we were walking to the parking garage, I told her not to watch for my car, because I came with Rachel. Mandy had to remind me that she was aware I didn't have my car since she was the one driving it. We laughed and laughed about that one!

Occasionally, when I would shop at a particular drug store, I would park in the same general area. On one of my visits, however, the lot was unusually full, and I had to park in a totally different location. I don't know how long I was in the store or what I was thinking when I came out, but I almost got into a car that was parked where I usually did. When I approached the car and was getting ready to open the door, I noticed someone sitting in it. As I was wondering who it was and why they were sitting in my car, I am sure the other person was wondering why I wanted to get in their vehicle. Thank goodness I realized my mistake before I actually opened the door. I found out that day that I wasn't the only person with a little red car who shopped at this drugstore.

I learned the hard way that if you use an air compressor to blow up a low tire, it must be plugged in first. Otherwise, as in my case, the rest of the air will come out of the tire.

I know it's not good when a wife mentions another man's name while dreaming. That's exactly what happened to me. I woke up one morning and Gordy asked me who Trevor Berbick was. I told him I didn't know. He said I was talking in my sleep and mentioned that name, as well as Zimbabwe. Just for fun, we looked up Trevor Berbick on the Internet. As it turns out, he was a real person—a well-known boxer. And he fought in Zimbabwe. Since I am not a fan of boxing, he was not so well known to me. I guess the boxing channel was on TV when I fell asleep. Yeah, that's it.

There was another incident that happened years ago when my kids were young. There used to be a commercial on TV about a mom who was rushing out the door to go to work to meet a client, and her daughter asked, "Mommy, when can I be a client?" I had dozed off on the couch when that commercial happened to come on and somehow that question got through to my brain. I raised up off the couch and said, "I don't know." Apparently, I am as scary when I'm asleep as I am when I'm awake!

How slow was I driving to get honked at in the cemetery? It happened.

When I am somewhere like the Smoky Mountains, I cannot ride the chair lift alone. For one thing, I feel like my feet are shrinking and my shoes are going to fall off. Another reason is because I feel like throwing something, like my purse or my camera. So for the safety of others, I have to have a riding companion so they can hold these things for me until I am back on the ground.

On one of my visits to the Smokies, I walked into a door of one store and later hit my head on the window of another. Yep, that's me.

Years ago I went to get my ears pierced at the mall. While it was being done, I heard screaming. I was told it was me, not the little girl who was also getting her ears pierced. I was thirty-five at the time.

I found out I don't function well with long nails. I had them done professionally for my wedding four years ago, and I thought I was going to put my eye out with them. My daughter also tried putting fake nails on me, and I ended up gluing my finger to hers. I guess I'll just stick with my little nubs.

I would rather ride an elevator with a serial killer than ride one by myself. I have been in situations where I will wait for another person to come along rather than ride alone. I have the fear of being stuck in one. If that ever happened, I would have to be rescued in two minutes or there would be no point. I would be even crazier than I am now. And I know I would never be able to climb up the cables like you see in the movies.

But I have problems with elevators even when I am with other people. Once I had someone hold one for me as I raced to get on I it. I stepped in, the "This car up" light went out, and we went nowhere. The elevator doors wouldn't even close. We all had to file out and get on another one. I've also been stepped on more than once while on an elevator. I always hear the same old line—"Oh, I'm sorry, I didn't see you."

One thing that has bothered me for years is my inability to French braid hair. I even bought an illustrated book with instructions when my girls were young, and I still couldn't master it. My daughter can French braid her own hair, and I am unable to do it on someone else. I must have two left feet for hands.

I volunteered one year to help at the Science Challenge at the local college. I was assigned to help with Logical Reasoning. Obviously, they didn't know me too well.

You may wonder how my family puts up with me. I had a coworker tell me once that if he was married to me, he wouldn't drink—he would go straight to drugs!

Car Troubles

Even when I get my car worked on, I experience the unusual. One time I took my vehicle in for an oil change and came home with a spare car part in the passenger seat that had nothing to do with the work I had done. I don't know what it was for, but apparently it wasn't important.

I needed new windshield wiper blades one time, so I took my vehicle to a car parts place to get replacements. One of the employees offered to put them on for me, and I accepted. He said there would be nothing to it. In my car's case, he was wrong. After several tries to get the old ones off, he had to get on top of my car to get the job done. He said he had never had that much trouble before. I wasn't surprised.

Another time I had a burned-out headlight and needed a new one. After going to three different places, I found the right one. Again, an employee offered to replace it for me. As he approached with the screwdriver to remove the old one, the headlight came on. I was beginning to think my car was possessed. I guess I would rather have it possessed than repossessed.

***

My car broke down one Sunday afternoon. I needed a tow and called a company that advertised as being open twenty-four hours a day, seven days a week. *Great,* I thought. *This is perfect.* When I called and explained my problem, the response I got was, "Sorry, we are closed."

"Closed?" I said. "Your ad says you are open twenty-four hours a day, seven days a week."

"We are," said the guy on the phone, "but this is our off day!"

***

When I worked downtown, I would park in a garage about two blocks from the building. One time I got to my office and realized I had locked my keys in my car. There was also a parking area in our building, so I went there and asked the security guard if he had any suggestions. He happened to have one of those devices that could reach through the car door and unlock it. I took him up on his offer to help me, and we made our way to the parking garage. As my luck would have it, the locks were such that the procedure did not work on my vehicle. The good news was I think I had the only car that could not be broken into. The bad news was my keys were still locked in the car. After wondering what to do next, the security guard was successful in unlocking the hatchback door. I didn't even mind climbing through the back to get my keys.

***

After having some work done on my car, I went to pick it up. I could see it in the parking lot as I went inside to pay the bill. The guy at the counter asked me for my name, shuffled some papers around, and then said, "Your car ain't here."

I said, "What do you mean, my car's not here?"

He said, "We ain't got no paperwork on it. If we don't have paperwork, we don't have your car."

"But I can see it from here. It's in your lot," was my response.

Again he basically said, no paperwork, no car. Finally, thank goodness, the paperwork was found. I'm not sure what I would have done if it weren't.

***

Several years ago, both of my vehicles had weather-related issues. My tiny car had a window that wouldn't go up because of the lift being broken, and my van's windshield wipers would only come on when they felt like it. I teasingly told my supervisor at work that I was a fair-weather employee because if it was raining, I would not be able to come to work. I couldn't believe both of my vehicles had a weather clause.

***

In the summer of 2013, I had to take my Saturn to the service station to get some transmission work done on it. When I was filling out the paperwork, I was told there was another Saturn there with the same problem. It turned out it was my son's car! We had both taken our Saturns to the same shop on the same day with the same problem.

***

I thought I lost my car keys one day, which would have been bad since I only had one key for the Saturn, which Gordy used, and one for the Miata. After searching frantically, I found my keys on the ground beside my car. Apparently, I had dropped them the day before. Because of that scare, I got duplicates made. Unfortunately, when I tried them, neither key worked!

Two days later, on Saturday, I took my van for what I thought was going to be just an oil change and tire rotation. It turned out to be a brake job too, so I had to leave it until that Monday. I was given a ride home, and then remembered my Miata key was also on the key ring at the shop. So I returned with the Saturn to get it so I wouldn't be without transportation when Gordy went to work on Monday. The smallest car used to have the biggest key—until now! I don't know what happened, but when my key ring was retrieved, the Miata key was about half its original size. How ironic that I just had keys made that wouldn't work, plus my only key to the Miata was broken. The shop was nice enough to send a locksmith to my house to make me a new key.

***

I even have issues when I just want to get gas for my car. I stopped once at a United Dairy Farmers and pumped gas then went into the store to pay for it. I gave the cashier my money, and when she was handing the change to me, it fell down the little hole where the cash register wire goes down into the counter. It must drop into a black hole, because it took awhile to get things dismantled and get the money out.

Another time I went to get gas for my car where there were two stations right next to each other. I went to the first one, but there were no pumps available. So I drove to the second one and completed my task. As I drove off, however, I did not realize that I had left my gas cap on top of my car until I heard it hit the pavement. I glanced in my rear view mirror and watched as it rolled down the middle of the street. It finally stopped in front of the first gas station. In the hopes of retrieving it, I drove back there. Just when I was about to step into the road to retrieve my gas cap, all I could do was watch helplessly as it was run over by a truck.

As I was pumping gas one very sunny day, there was a glare so that I could not read the numbers being displayed. I wanted to make sure the gas was really going into my car, so I pulled the nozzle of the pump out slightly to see. That was a mistake. Gas ran up my coat sleeve, and I smelled like an accident waiting to happen. When I went inside to pay my bill, they couldn't get me out fast enough. I'm just glad no one lighted a cigarette or something, or I would have been history.

Even when I am in a car accident, there are weird circumstances. Years ago I had taken my daughters to the dentist, and we were heading home on a rainy evening. We were going down a winding road, and I slid and hit another vehicle coming the opposite direction. Rachel made the comment that the girl in the other car looked familiar. As it turned out, she was in my daughter's Girl Scout troop. Not only that, but her parents had just purchased the car a few days earlier. Needless to say, they were not too happy with me. We were taken to the hospital as a precaution. I had to have my knee x-rayed, since it was hurting badly. Of course, the first x-ray machine was not operating correctly. On top of that, Rachel had a perfect report from the dentist but ended up having to have a root canal because of the accident.

More Funny Stuff

I have a mother's ring with the birthstones of my three children. I had it for several years when one of the birthstones fell out and I had to have it replaced. The store where the ring was purchased ended up replacing the ring, which was great. What wasn't great was the fact that when I picked it up, one of the birthstones was wrong.

Everyone has those chores that we keep putting off. One of mine is cleaning out closets. I never know what I will find. One time while cleaning my bedroom closet, I found my maternity clothes (my youngest child was eighteen at the time) and an air filter for a truck I hadn't had for ten years. I'm still trying to figure out what the air filter was doing in my bedroom. In another closest, I found a Red Lobster gift card that I had received when I retired six years earlier, my second key clicker for my car, and one of Mandy's birthday cards that still had her birthday money in it from years earlier.

Something else that was not high on my priority list was cleaning out my car. One day a friend found a dead taco under the passenger seat. And once I even found my completed tax returns from the previous year. The good news was, if I ever had to live out of my car, I probably could have. But I am happy to say that in recent years, I have gotten better at keeping my car clean. Now I don't have to worry about getting hurt by flying debris.

One day I finally found that library book that was three years overdue. I went to turn it in and was told that I had reached the maximum allowable limit for book fines. I was afraid to ask how much it was because I thought I was going to have to whip out my credit card to pay for it. Were they going to throw the book at me? It ended up being a big $2.30. I was relieved. I had that much change in the bottom of my purse.

I ordered a Mother's Day cake for my mom one year. When I got it home and looked at it, it didn't say Happy Mother's Day, but Happy Mothday Day. Doesn't that take the cake.

***

It was April Fool's Day one year, and my daughters thought it would be fun to terrorize their mom. I experienced everything from plastic on the toilet seat to having Vaseline-coated cotton balls under my car door handle. I scare easily anyway, and I thought I was going to have a heart attack before I made it out the door to go to work.

I got back at Rachel one year for the tricks she played on me. When she was thirteen, she had a huge crush on the group Hanson. (She still does.)

There was a contest being held to win backstage tickets to their upcoming show in Orlando, Florida. I typed up a letter stating that she was the lucky winner and mailed it to her. I signed the letter R. U. Fooled. Well, somehow she figured out it was a joke, and I didn't fool her at all. But I had fun trying anyway.

About that same time, I did take Rachel and Mandy to a Hanson concert at Riverbend in Cincinnati. It was outside, and my daughters did not have tickets for seating, but rather for standing outside of the fence. Rachel's hands were so intertwined in the fence that I wasn't sure I was going to be able to free her once the concert was over. Mandy was almost as bad. I don't think either one had much of a voice the next day.

***

I called the Cincinnati Bell Anytime Line one day and got a message telling me that it was not available, and I should call back later. I guess it's anytime but that time.

Sometimes I'm just at the wrong place at the wrong time—and I include other people! One spring day in 2013, Gordy and I went to lunch with his mom and sister. We were driving home from the restaurant when suddenly we heard a loud pop. As we soon discovered, the windshield of our vehicle had been shot out by a gun—a caulking gun—that flew out of the side of the lawnmower of a homeowner who happened to be mowing their grass. As I said—wrong place at the wrong time.

CHAPTER 6

THAT'S JUST SICK

I know it's just psychological, but I have always had a hard time swallowing pills. I went to the doctor one time and needed a prescription. When he asked me if I preferred pills or liquid, I said liquid. "Too bad," he said, "Pills are all we have."

Years ago, I was hospitalized with pneumonia. After being there for several days, I finally started feeling well enough to take a shower. I asked if it was okay for my family to bring my blow dryer for my hair. I was told, "Yes, but don't use it in the shower." Would I have lived as long as I have if I didn't know that already?

One day, for no good reason, I slammed my finger in the deadbolt lock on my back door. Even though this happened years ago, I still cringe at the thought of it. Of all my fingers, it had to be my middle one that was injured. After it got stitched and wrapped at the emergency room, it was huge. Whenever I was driving, I felt like people thought I was being offensive to them. About a week after the incident, I fell down my steps, and my son came to my aid. He heard me say, "Ouch ouch ouch." He asked me if I hurt something in my fall, and I told him no, he was standing on my finger—the same one I had slammed in the lock!

***

Years ago, I had to have surgery, and I was a little nervous about it. I always have the fear of not waking up from the anesthesia. One of my coworkers didn't help when he told me to say hello to his grandmother. I asked him if she worked at the hospital, and he said "No, she's dead." Not very encouraging. I wanted to wake up to flowers, not a toe tag.

I did make it through the surgery, but when I woke up, my husband wasn't the first person I saw. It was a male coworker. That was weird. It was also weird that there were drapes in my room, but no real window. And a man came in looking for a broom. I was beginning to think that I was really in some sort of closet. That would be about right. The treatment I received wasn't what I expected either. I didn't have pain medicine going into my IV, as I had been told would happen. Instead I would get a shot in the rear whenever I needed pain relief. I was also forgotten when it came to meals.

One of the treatments I had to do once I got home was soak in a saltwater solution. I have never heard anyone else doing this, but the doctor told my husband he could go to the pet shop and get what I needed. We only needed a small amount. So my husband Eddie went to the pet store, hoping to be discreet, and made his request. He said they did not understand why he wanted such a little bit, and they kept telling him it was not enough for an aquarium. So much for being discreet!

***

I was twenty-nine when I got braces on my teeth. I still had them at age thirty-three, when my daughter, Rachel, was born. I was playing with her on the floor one day, and I got my braces stuck to her shirt. My husband had to get me loose.

It was fun going to the orthodontist and trying to bond with kids half my age. It was like an assembly line of dental chairs, and we would all be sitting there, waiting our turn. The kids were nice, and they would try to talk to me to help pass the time, but what did I have in common with them? They had homework; I had housework. They babysat; I had a baby They would whine; I drank wine. I'm sure I seemed ancient to them.

The braces turned out to be not enough to fix my problem, and I had to have my jaw broken and realigned. After the surgery, my jaw was wired shut for about eight weeks, which meant I was on a liquid diet. During this time, I noticed that people who never wanted to talk to me before wanted to talk to me then.

My Thanksgiving meal that year came out of a blender. The most important thing I learned from that experience was not to put green beans in the blender first. The result was various shades of green for everything else that went in the blender, which sort of ruined everyone else's appetite.

One time while on my liquid diet, I stopped at Kentucky Fried Chicken and only ordered side dishes. After I placed my order, the cashier asked, "Don't you want any chicken with that?"

The day finally came when I found out there was life after braces. When they came off, I got a permanent retainer, which broke one day at lunch while eating killer tuna salad.

***

I always get novocaine when I have dental work done. During one visit I needed two small fillings and was given novocaine to numb things up. Well, shot number one did not work. I could feel the drill. Shot number two was a repeat of number one. When I was given the third shot of novocaine, I did get numb, but my legs began to feel funny and my heart started racing. I told my dentist, and he assured me it was nothing to worry about. Then the next thing I heard was, "Bring the oxygen!" I have always wondered where novocaine goes when it doesn't work. It went somewhere in my body. Will I be driving down the street someday and have my arm go limp and be unable to steer my car? Or maybe my leg will go numb, and I will just fall to the ground? I worry about things like that.

One time I had to get a tooth implant. Before starting the procedure, the dentist took my blood pressure and said my heart rate was up. That wasn't surprising. After all, I was getting ready to have a metal spike driven into my mouth.

I used to think my purpose in life was to make my dentist rich. I should be the queen of something with all the crowns I have. Or at the very least I should have a chair named after me. Every time I go to the dentist, I have something that needs to be done. At my age, you would think I would have outgrown cavities. On the rare occasion when I get a good report, it makes me want to come home and eat a whole bowl of sugar.

Even if I get out of the dentist's office without pain, that doesn't mean I will get home without it. One time after leaving the dentist's office, I slammed my thumb in my car door.

CHAPTER 7

SENIOR MOMENTS

Everything changes as we grow older. I used to have an hourglass figure. Now I have the whole clock. When I go into a public restroom where there are hand dryers, I used to have to put my hands under them to get them to come on. Now all I have to do is walk past them. That's not good. I have seen myself in a whole new light. It just takes more lights now.

I got some surprising news when I went for a checkup and found out I am five foot five. I told the doctor that couldn't be true because my whole adult life I was told I was five foot four. In fact, even my driver's license said I was five foot four, and everyone knows that information is always 100 percent accurate. The doctor measured me again, and sure enough I am five foot five. So instead of shrinking in my old age, I must be getting taller. Either that, or I've been a liar all these years. The good thing is, with that extra inch to play with, my weight doesn't seem so bad now. The bad news is, if I keep growing like this, by the time I am seventy, I will be seven feet tall.

The truth hurts sometimes. I went to the eye doctor a while back because I was seeing spots. I thought I had something wrong with my eyes, but he assured me that wasn't the case. He told me I was just getting old.

Some people never know the exact moment when they realize they are getting old. I did. My moment was when my supervisor at work was younger than my son. That should never happen. I had clothes older than he was.

***

I have to mention gray hair for a moment. Sooner or later it happens. For me it was sooner. By the time I was thirty, my salt-and-pepper hair was mainly salt. I dyed my hair for years, until I decided I needed all my brain cells more than I needed brown hair. One time I was between hair colors when my driver's license came up for renewal. The woman waiting on me took one look at my hair and decided to call it "mixed." I told her that was not happening, and I was not going through the next four years with that on my license. She could pick a color—gray or brown—I didn't care. Otherwise, it made me sound like a mixed-breed dog or something. She picked brown.

***

One time I had my four-year-old daughter at a neighborhood pool. I was minding my own business when a little girl about five came near me and asked in a sweet little voice, "Are you a mommy?"

And I said, "Well, yes I am. There is my little girl right over there," and I pointed toward my daughter's direction.

At that, the girl said in a not-so-sweet voice, "Oh. You had so much gray hair I thought you were a grandma!" With that she turned and swam away.

***

A similar incident happened when my children were small and I stopped at our local grocery store on my way home from work. About the same time I was entering the store, a father and his young son were coming in too. The son was pushing one of those kiddie grocery carts, and he wasn't paying attention. When he almost hit me with it, I heard the father say, "Watch out. You almost knocked over that little old lady." If I had had an AARP card, I would have beat him with it.

***

Years ago I dropped off a roll of film to be developed. When I came back for my pictures, the girl behind the counter was flipping through them with her young, teenage hands and said, "These kids are cute. Are they your grandchildren?" Again an AARP card would have come in handy!

I went to lunch one time at a steakhouse, and they automatically charged me for the Senior Citizen Special. I was thirty-five at the time. I must have had a really bad day at work, or else my gray hair was peeking through again. Time to hit the bottle!

One summer I spent a week at 4-H horse camp with Mandy and our miniature horse, Buddy. After sleeping in a tent for five nights, I was comparing myself to the old gray mare because I knew I ain't what I used to be. After a few nights, I was lucky I could walk in an upright position.

I have found that I am a little more forgetful than I used to be. I used to know the Gettysburg address; now I'm lucky to know my own. After a trip to the grocery store, I paid for my groceries but walked away without them. The bad thing was I didn't even realize I was pushing an empty cart until I heard the cashier say, "Hey, lady, don't you want your groceries?" I guess I got distracted talking to the people in front of me. My multitasking skills aren't as sharp as they used to be.

There comes a time in a parent's life when we become more like children, and the children become more like parents. Several years ago, my kids got me the Nintendo Wii for Christmas. It came with a warning—and I don't mean the one from the manufacturer. This one was from my children. They told me if I hurt myself or couldn't move the next day from playing, they were going to pull the plug. So I must play with caution.

A few years ago, my sister-in-law had a chick party at her house. It was really an old hen party. We talked about our new friends—Ben Gay, Arthur Ritis, Gerry Tall, Nita Cane, and Harry Chin.

Garbage pickup is on Thursdays for me. One week I forgot to set it out. I wasn't going to let that happen again. The following week, I meant to put it out the night before collection day, but it slipped my mind. I went to bed worrying about it. I decided to set my alarm clock so I would not miss it. The next morning, I got up early, dragged my garbage out to the curb, and noticed no one else had theirs out. I was a day early!

Once I was a whole week early for a meeting at church and a day early for another one. It's not fun getting old and confused.

***

In 2010, I bought a sporty little 1992 Mazda Miata. It was old but cute. My son was fine with it, but my daughters questioned my sanity, even though I kept telling them was going to get a little convertible once I retired. I thought that plan was on hold because of my upcoming marriage to Gordy, but the car was too cute to pass up (just like Gordy!). Rachel wanted to know if I needed intervention. In her view, I was going through a midlife crisis. Mandy's comment was "Mom, I leave you alone for a year, and look what you do." Just because I'm old doesn't mean I can't have fun, and that car sure is fun to drive. And it's almost too much cuteness when Gordy drives it. It's as sweet as a sugar high.

***

In 2014, my grandson, Adam, had his eighth birthday party at a roller skating rink. I was the first grandparent who was brave or crazy enough to strap on a pair of roller skates and go out on the rink. I did well for a while. In fact, my daughter was calling me a speed demon. Then my luck ran out. I don't know what happened, but one minute I was up, and the next I was down. The good news is that I was told I fell gracefully. The bad news is I fell on my right hand, and I happen to be right handed. When it began hurting immediately, I knew that was going to be an issue once I got home. But I didn't let it mess up the evening. I even continued to skate.

Later everyone went to the party room, where we enjoyed cake and ice cream and watched as Adam opened his presents. During this time, my daughter, Rachel, and I were sitting at the end of one of the tables near one of Adam's friends. The little boy was very friendly, and he and Rachel began a conversation about how they both love chocolate. Suddenly, out of the blue, the boy turned to me and asked, "So, how old are you?" I was so stunned I answered him honestly. His response was "Wow!" My daughter told me later I could have said I was thirty-five because that seems ancient to an eight-year-old too.

As we left the roller rink, I was looking forward to getting home and putting ice on my poor hand. But I had to drive home first—and my car is a stick. Ouch. It was painful to shift, but I finally made it home. I could barely move my wrist at that point. In fact, when I brushed my teeth that night, I had to hold the brush still while I shook my head back and forth. My left hand just wasn't ready to take over that task.

Retirement

In 2006, after thirty-two years of employment at Duke Energy, I got the chance to retire early. Once that decision was finalized, I started bringing baked treats to work every Monday. It was a great thing, because if I saw a new recipe I wasn't too sure about, I could try it out on my coworkers before I served it to my family. After a few weeks, I had everyone spoiled. I started having my own welcoming committee. I worked at a construction office, and most of the people there were guys. It was funny seeing them lurking around the door and looking for me each Monday. They seemed to like everything I brought in. In fact, I began to worry they would like it so much that they would get too out of shape to climb poles anymore. I didn't need that to happen. After all, I didn't want the value of my stock to go down. But I continued to bring in treats, and they continued to like them. Once I brought in some cookies called snickerdoodles. They were a big hit, especially with one particular guy. In fact, he wanted me to bring in some more of those "Shag Nasties," as he called them. He never did get the name right. I don't know about anyone else, but I wouldn't eat anything called a "Shag Nasty." I brought treats in all the way up to my last day, and they asked if I was going to continue after that. I told them sorry, but no, and don't call me at home and expect to hear a recording like, "If you want cookies, press 1; if you want cake press 2."

Believe it or not, my computer at work was upgraded six days before I retired. That meant I needed to create and use a new password for the last three days of my employment.

There were eight of us from my department who were retiring on the same day, so we were given one big party. When I walked into the reception room, everything was decorated beautifully, and we each had our own table to set up with our personal items. It was nice having our families there as well. I was hoping the day would go smoothly with no mishaps. I should have known better. I had just arrived, and as I was leaning down to put my purse under my table, I felt something hit me in the head. I thought I was going to be knocked out and miss my own party. I soon discovered the source of my pain was an elbow to the head by my own daughter.

I thought this would be the end of my bad luck for the day. That was before my sister informed me about the cake. It was supposed to have the first and last names of the eight retirees, which was true for the other seven. My first name wasn't on it at all, and my last name was misspelled. But I didn't care how or even if my name was on the cake—that wasn't going to keep me from retiring.

As the party went on, my daughter, Rachel, was going to use my camera to get a picture of everyone as we retirees stood in line to be presented with a gift. Well, there were a few seconds of delay between the time the button was pushed and the time the picture was actually taken. In that tiny time-frame, a man walked exactly in front of where I was standing. As a result, I wasn't even in the picture.

One thing I didn't have to worry about was my family knowing where I was during the party. I did what became known as my retirement dance where I would say a little "woo-hoo!" and my arms would go up in the air. So whenever they lost me in the crowd, all they had to do was watch for the arms, and there I was.

In addition to the gift we received at the party, we got another one in the mail. Mine came addressed not to Sharon Witherington, but to Sharon Washington. I thought that after thirty-two years, they would have my name correct. Although I did have a supervisor who never got my first name right. He called me Shirley for four years.

***

Of course, after thirty-two years of employment, there were plenty of funny stories. I don't know anyone who had to be driven to work by a state trooper—except for me. My day started as usual. I was driving my daughters, ages one and three at the time, to the sitter's on my way to work. I noticed that I slid a little bit going around a turn near my house, but I thought it was because the road was a little slick from the rain we had that morning. I continued on my way, until I felt and heard one side of my car thumping as I was going up the hill on the highway. So I pulled over to an emergency stop area and found my rear tire flatter than a pancake. Apparently, I had run over a nail.

I didn't know what I was going to do. After I had sat there for about ten minutes, a guy in a van stopped and called the state police. A few minutes later, a young state trooper came and tried to fix my flat, but he couldn't find my jack. I did have one, but it was in a hidden compartment. Apparently very well hidden! His jack would not fix my car.

The officer offered to drive me and the girls to the sitter's and me to work. I accepted his offer, and we transferred the car seats and kids to his vehicle. He carried my daughter, Mandy, to his car, and either he squeezed her too hard or she was scared, because she peed on him. He was so nice that he took us to the sitter's anyway. After dropping off the children, the trooper drove me to work. I told him to take me around to the back door of the building, hoping to slip in without having to explain my means of transportation. Unfortunately, a coworker was coming in just as the police car arrived with me in it. Boy, did I get teased all day about that! Later two of my coworkers returned to the scene of the flat and put the temporary tire on for me, and I was able to drive it home. My babysitter told me later that she didn't know what to think when she saw the police pulling into her driveway that morning.

***

Another time on my way to work, I ran over a muffler in the road and got another flat tire. I got teased about that too. I didn't understand that. After all, I didn't run over *my own* muffler.

When I turned forty, my coworkers surprised me with a cake and some "presents," which included a cane, dark glasses, a Fortyland T-shirt (where the fun never starts), and some other "old people" items. The cake was perfect for the occasion, with black icing, a vulture, and candles that couldn't be blown out. In fact, the cake almost turned into a fireball when we couldn't extinguish the candles. We ended up having to put the cake outside by the door. The UPS man happened to come with a delivery that day, and he did a double take when he walked past it to get in the building. It was a hot, melty mess.

In that same office, all the clerical personnel sat in one area. There was Phyllis, Madeline, me, and Debbie. If you took the first initial of our names you got PMS'D. That explained a lot!

I don't know what it was about attending meetings, but I always had an unusual story. Years ago I had to attend an all-day seminar that was going to be held at a hotel in downtown Cincinnati. First I got tied up in some traffic because of an accident on the highway, and I was afraid I was going to be late. Then I got turned around after I parked my car and had to ask a taxi driver for directions to the hotel. Once I got to the hotel, I was sent to the wrong conference room. I was there with two other people from my work for quite some time before we realized we were in the wrong place. I think we were in the middle of a truck drivers' convention. But it wasn't all bad—their donuts were good. Once we got to the right room and ate more donuts, things got better, although I was number thirteen to sign in.

I had to go to an informal departmental meeting for work one time, which was held at a big conference room at a reception center. We were sitting in groups of twelve at round tables before the meeting started, and there was a little ball being tossed back and forth among the tables. No one had a problem with it—until it came to me. The ball hit me in the head and landed in our pitcher of water, causing a splash that resulted in a wet table.

One time I had to fill in at another district for someone who was on vacation. I had never worked at this office before so I wasn't even sure where to enter the building. After parking my car, I saw a group of employees walking towards the building. So I followed them—right into the men's locker room. It wouldn't have been too bad except I was told it took me fifteen minutes to come back out. Well, what can I say—I wanted to make sure I was really in the wrong place.

There was a group of us were returning from lunch one winter day when there was snow on the ground. One of the guys picked up some and casually tossed it over his shoulder without looking. I was behind him, and the snowball hit me in my face. Thank goodness I had sunglasses on.

Once I was mistaken for a coworker—which wouldn't have been bad if he weren't a guy. We both had short hair and glasses at the time.

Years ago I had a supervisor who asked me if I had a previous job as a gargoyle. He said I could sit motionless for hours and give people evil looks.

When I became a grandma, it was announced in the "people news" at work that I had a beautiful new granddaughter. Unfortunately, that was not quite right, since that was when my grandson was born.

The last place that I worked before I retired was a construction office. I don't remember what I got upset with the guys about regarding their paperwork, but I decided to write a message on the whiteboard in their break room. By the time I got out there, I was so upset that I grabbed the first marker I could find and began writing. I knew I was over the edge, because it was reflected in my penmanship. Some of the letters were big, and some of the letters were small. It looked like a ransom note. When I finished, I took a look at it and decided to rewrite it so it wouldn't look so psychotic. To my surprise, I couldn't erase it. I had used the permanent marker.

Life after Duke

Shortly after I retired, I was looking for something fun to do. I decided to take beginner line dancing lessons at a nearby senior center. I wasn't fifty-five yet, but the eighty-three-year-old instructor said I could take the class anyway. Everyone else was at least twenty to twenty-five years older than me, and I was referred to as "the new girl." The lessons began, and I attended for several weeks. I knew I needed a lot of help, but I did not realize how bad I was until the day I was approached by the instructor.

She said, "Sharon, I know you are trying really hard, but you need to start coming in twenty minutes early and get some one on one help." She went on to say, "You're slowing down the class." So I wasn't keeping up with the eighty-year-olds. Apparently I was the poster child for bad line dancing. That was it for me. I turned in my dancing shoes. I was afraid if I went back after that, I would see my picture on the door with a slash through it.

***

Something else I did after I retired was sign up for a quilting class. I took it to not only fill some time, but also relieve my stress. It did fill my time, but it definitely did not relieve my stress. In fact, I think I needed a quilting support group. When I got ready to put the back on my quilt, it was not lining up right, so I had to go to class four hours early one day to get some help. I didn't get done until five that afternoon, and the class started at six, so basically I was at my quilting class from two to nine. I finally did finish my one and only quilt. I don't think I will be back to that class again, unless they have one where they make coasters. Maybe I could handle that.

***

In 2008, I answered an ad to work at HoneyBaked Ham for Easter week. I ended up working there part-time for five years. As I soon learned, some hams are butts and some are shanks. Shortly after I started, I remember waiting on a man who said he wanted "a nice big butt." Then he kind of smiled said he couldn't believe he was talking that way to a lady. It really is the only place where you can talk about nice butts and not get in trouble.

At HoneyBaked Ham, everyone works more hours around the holidays, and sometimes it gets a little crazy. I had seen so many hams that one Christmas, I didn't even remember taking one to my sister-in-law's a few days before. We were having dinner at her house, and I asked who brought the ham. I was told I did. Without thinking, I told a friend of mine that Easter keeps us hopping.

Not everyone understands my humor. My manager at HoneyBaked always wore festive hats during the holidays. It was nearing Christmas one year, and she had on a hat that looked like a Christmas tree with lights on it. I asked her if she felt "lightheaded." She said, "No, I feel pretty good today."

I sold about five chickens one day within the first thirty minutes of opening the store. I told my manager we needed some more because they were flying off the shelves.

One day I was making phone calls to local businesses telling them about the catering menu. After doing this for a good part of the day, I think I started to sound a bit animated. When I made one of my calls, I relayed all the pertinent information and waited for a response. What I got was silence. A moment later, the lady on the other end asked, "Is this a recording?" I wondered why she would ask such a question. If it were a recording, was she expecting to hear "Well, yes it is! How did you know?"

Deliveries can be tricky sometimes. This one was in downtown Cincinnati. I had to take six boxes of food to the fourteenth floor of an office building. It was one problem after another getting the delivery done. The parking garage was full, so I had to drive around the block a few times waiting for a parking spot to open. After that, I took the heaviest box across the street and into the lobby, only to have to take it back to the van and drive around to the loading dock in the back of the building. The security officer there offered me no assistance when I had to push the big red button on the wall to open the security doors with my arms full of boxes.

When preparing for another delivery, I almost put the order in a customer's vehicle instead of HoneyBaked Ham's. They had a white van that looked just like ours. I was wondering why there were wrapped packages in the back of it. Fortunately, I realized my mistake before it got too embarrassing.

I scraped my knuckle while loading the boxes for another delivery. It was just a scratch, and I thought nothing more about it. However, while driving I managed to get those two drops of blood on the sleeve of my brand new jacket.

A heart and vascular center was where I had to make another delivery. It was a large order that involved a lot of boxes. It was nice to know where that facility was located, because after that delivery, I thought I might need their services.

One time I had just finished making sandwiches for a big order when a customer walked into the store. While talking to him, I was trying to carry a tray of wrapped sandwiches over to the lunch boxes. Just as I passed the trash can, two of them slid in. Proof that I can't walk and talk at the same time.

I was reaching up to get the big box of cheese off the shelf when a one-pound package of it slid off and hit me in the head. Fortunately, there were no witnesses to this cheesy incident.

For almost a week I couldn't find my magnetic name tag. Then I went to the post office to get my mail. Low and behold, it was in my mailbox. It must have attached itself to my key when I got it out of my purse and then dropped on the floor. Someone found it, turned it in, and the postmaster put it in my box. I couldn't believe it.

I was working at HoneyBaked Ham when I got married to Gordy and received the ultimate acknowledgment. An announcement about the event was put in the *Pigmania Press*, which is HoneyBaked Ham's newsletter. How do I top that?

Our computer program was updated, and all the employees had to sign in and get set up. When I did, I got the following message: *Welcome Sharon Hickey. You are a terminated employee.* Was I the last to know something important? Did I miss an opportunity to sleep in?

Most of the time I didn't have to close, but one Saturday I did. So I mopped the floor and was trying to dump the mop water when the big bucket got away from me. I thought I hung up the mop, but somehow in the commotion, it fell out of the hook in the closet and hit me in the head. My left ear was fiery red. That's the ear that has always given me trouble over the years. Anyway, I don't know if I knocked something back in place or if I knocked something loose, but I think I can hear better out of it now. Not only did I hit myself in the head, but I spilled mop water all over the hallway. It looked like a mini river. With the help of my manager, we used the big water sucker thing to get it cleaned up.

***

If there ever was a perfect example of a bad day, this next story is it. I was getting ready to leave for HoneyBaked Ham one morning. When I opened the door that leads down to my garage, my kittens were trying to run down the stairs. Since I did not want them to do that, I bent down to push them away from the door and struck my forehead on the doorknob. I almost gave a hickey to a Hickey! After seeing stars for a few moments, I continued on with my day and went to work.

I'm going to blame these next few events on my head injury. After being at work for a little while, I noticed that our little oven was beginning to smoke. Without remembering that I had put bacon in it, I asked my coworkers what was going on. Then I realized it was me who had caused the problem. Thank goodness we got the store desmoked before the sprinklers came on.

I thought that would be the end of my bad day, but I should have known better. After working my usual four hours, I left to come home. I went out to the parking lot, tried to start my car, and discovered I had left my headlights on. I had a dead battery. No one at work had battery cables, and mine were at home. So I walked across the street to a car-rental place, and they had some they were willing to let me borrow. No one there was able to leave the workplace, but fortunately, one of my female coworkers knew how to jump my car. In a few minutes my battery was all charged. She then told me it would be a good idea to keep the car running for a few minutes. I agreed and said, "Okay, you watch my car, and I will take these cables back." So without thinking that I could drive there, I left her with my car while I walked back to the car-rental place.

I was hoping my bad day was finally over. It wasn't. I had to take my kittens to the vet that afternoon, and on the way I remembered I needed cat food. So I stopped at the store and purchased some. I paid for the food, but then I walked out without it.

When I went to bed that night, I was sure my troubles were over. I was wrong. At three in the morning, I got up to use the restroom, which meant going down three steps to a small landing. Somehow I missed them all. As a result, I fell onto the linoleum floor on my knee. It hurt so bad that I could not get up, so I started yelling for Gordy. It took him awhile to get to me, even though this happened right outside our bedroom door. He later told me the reason he wasn't in a hurry was because he thought I had just found my fifteen-year-old dog dead. In any case, he helped me up. I then remember saying that I felt like I was going to pass out. And sure enough, I did, even though it was only for a minute or two.

That freaked us both out, so I took Gordy's advice and got checked out by the doctor. One of the things he asked me was if I had had any other forgetful episodes since that day. I told him no, that I was fine. (Would I remember if I did?) After telling the doctor that I had no other incidents, I went home and found a message on my answering machine. It said I had forgotten my medical cards at the doctor's office. I think I had a case of COL—Crazy Old Lady! This experience wasn't all bad. Right after it all happened, Gordy got me a new smartphone to replace my old flip phone. I guess he thought if something happened to me, at least I would go out in style!

***

As 2013 was nearing an end, I decided to turn in my apron at HoneyBaked Ham and direct my time and effort to this book. It was almost Christmas, and I wanted to make a cheesecake to share with my friends there. I used my silicone springform pan, which I have done many other times with no problem. As I was getting it out of the oven this time, however, somehow the sides of the pan stretched, and the bottom fell out. The result was not pretty. I had cheesecake everywhere, including in the oven, on the oven, on the floor, and on the wall. I was so upset. It was too late to make another one, so I was going to have to go to work the next day without it. Gordy was so nice to help me clean up the mess. He even took off the oven door so we could better clean it. Good intentions turned out to be a mistake, though. No matter how hard we tried, we could not get the oven door back on. Normally they click right back on—but not mine. It was going to be Christmas Eve in just a few days, and all my family was coming over for dinner. We had to do something about that door. After trying unsuccessfully for an hour to reattach the door, we finally gave up. I had to call an appliance repairman to get the problem resolved. It cost us more than one hundred dollars. That was one expensive cheesecake that no one got to eat.

***

While I worked at HoneyBaked Ham, I also worked part-time in a small office for about a year. My main responsibility was to balance bank statements. I thought this was ironic, since I hadn't balanced my own checking account in more than twenty years.

Upon entering the office building with a pass, there was an alarm system that had to be turned off within a certain amount of time and then set again when leaving for the day. If this procedure was not followed correctly, the police would be notified by security. Sometimes the office was cold, and I had a heater under my desk that I would turn on if necessary. One Friday I left the office for the day. Later that evening, I remembered that I had not turned off the heater. Since I didn't want to be responsible for possibly causing a fire, I had to find out how to get back into the building without setting off the alarm. I had to call my supervisor, who happened to be home recuperating from recent surgery, for instructions. There was a keypad outside the main door, and she told me I could get in with my pass. When I tried that, however, I discovered I also needed a code, which I didn't have. So I had to call her a second time. I felt terrible because I could tell she was still in a medicated state when I was talking to her. I finally got in the building, disarmed the security system, unplugged the heater, and reset the alarm. And I got out of the building without having the police notified. Hooray!

My workstation was in the front of the office. There was a betta fish named Jack whose home was on the counter just above my desk. The security alarm was also on that counter and very close to the fishbowl. More than once I accidentally set it off. Poor Jack! I am sure during these times he thought he was *fin*ished. At least that was the kind of look he gave me.

***

After hearing many of my stories, a friend asked me if my luck is always like this. I said, "No, sometimes it's bad."

AFTERWORD

So there you have it—my true, funny stories. If I hadn't lived through them myself, I may not have believed them. The next time someone thinks she's having an off day or has a bad experience in a restaurant, I hope she thinks about me. Maybe she will feel better. And if there's somebody out there who had his shoes catch on fire during a concert, I hope I find out about it so I'll know I'm not alone. These experiences have taught me patience, forgiveness, and, most of all, the importance of having a sense of humor. After all, it's either laugh or cry.

***

There is just one more thing to add. On April Fool's Day 2014, I tried to submit my material for this book for publication. With my luck, I should have known better than try to do something important on this particular day. It started out with technical difficulties when my computer would not open the CD that my material was on. My second computer did open the CD, but it had no antivirus program on it, so I was hesitant to send it over the Internet. To be safe, I decided to take that second computer to our local computer repair shop and have the antivirus installed. I arrived before their business hours, so I decided to take the CD, which I had with me, to our local library and use one of their computers. It came as no surprise when I encountered road construction and a detour that took me the long way around. It didn't matter, because when I finally got to the library, it was closed.

So I went back home and waited for the computer shop to open. I returned an hour later to find the Open sign on, but the door was locked, and no one was there. So I used my cell phone to call and leave a message. From there I decided to go to an electronics store to have the antivirus program installed on my computer. On the way there, I got a call from the computer repair shop telling me it would be three more hours before someone would be there. I went ahead and got the program installed at the electronics store and then went to another library to submit my material from the CD. I accessed the Internet from one of their computers and thought I would finally be able to complete my mission. I was wrong. The publisher's website was down! It could only happen to me!

CPSIA information can be obtained at www.ICGtesting.com
Printed in the USA
BVOW07*1934090315

390937BV00001B/2/P